killer technique®

hammered dulcimer

by dr. mark alan wade

WWW.MELBAY.COM

Table of Contents

Introduction

Killer Technique: Hammered Dulcimer is a daily practice routine book inspired by Corey Christiansen's *Gig Savers: Killer Technique* book for guitar (MB#20028). This book provides concepts and daily studies to help players gain facility on their instrument by improving hammer technique and refining key rudiments and patterns. As such, it is useful for all levels of musicians. This book is written to accommodate dulcimers from a 12/11 size through extended range and chromatic instruments. Some exercises may begin lower than the range of a 12/11, but continue up into that range. For best results, work on the exercises in the entire playable range of your instrument.

This book begins with exercises that will improve your actual hammer grip, aim and playing technique. The second section presents percussion rudiments that will improve hammer control and are commonly used as embellishments. The final section is devoted to reinforcing the most commonly used chord patterns on the instrument. These exercises, like any physical exercises, should be tackled slowly at first; tempo can gradually be increased over time. This will ensure proper technique is employed from the beginning. This book can be used as a daily warm-up or as a means to advance to the next level in your musicianship. Strive to master these exercises with a metronome and you will find that there will not be much out there that you can't play on the dulcimer!

The Anatomy of the Hammered Dulcimer

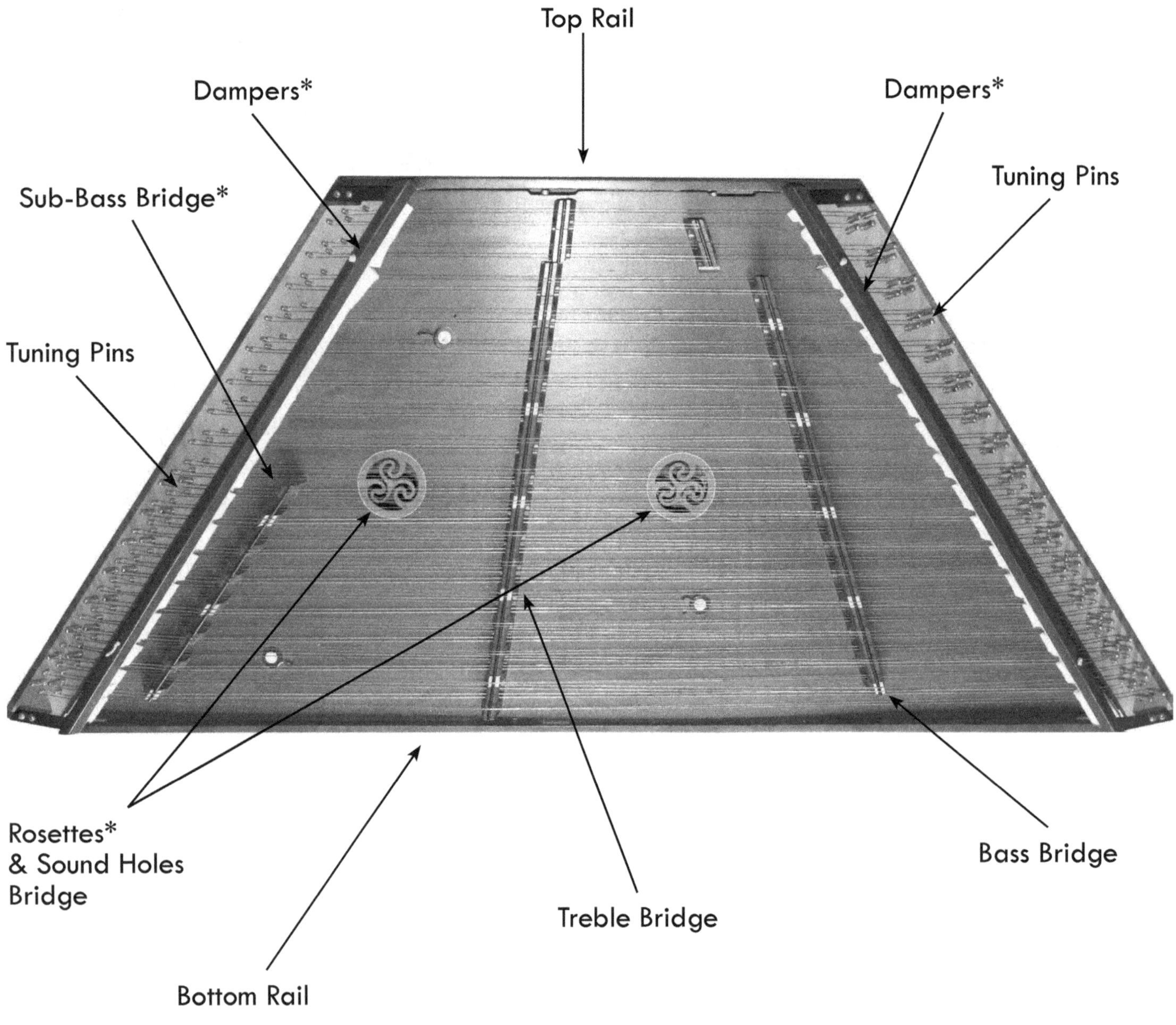

This dulcimer is a ~Cloud Nine~ 17/16/8 made by Michael C. Allen, Ostrander, Ohio, with dampers and triple-spiral rosettes in the sound holes.
*Denotes optional features.

Hammer Grip

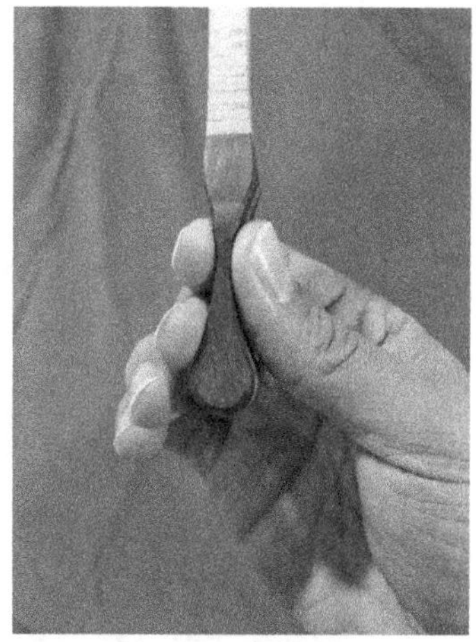

Active Grip

For all-around playing, keep those middle fingers in contact with the hammer! Also called the "Two-Finger Grip," the index finger and the middle finger hold the bottom of the hammer (hence, "two-finger") and the thumb is on top. This is an active grip because the fingers of the grip themselves produce the motion. In this hold, the index finger is the fulcrum and the middle finger is like a trigger to initiate the strike. The continuing motion comes from your fingers offsetting the weight of the hammer heads and the rebound from the strings–not from your elbow. The middle finger is partnered with the thumb in springing back against the hammer motion and redirecting it to the next strike.

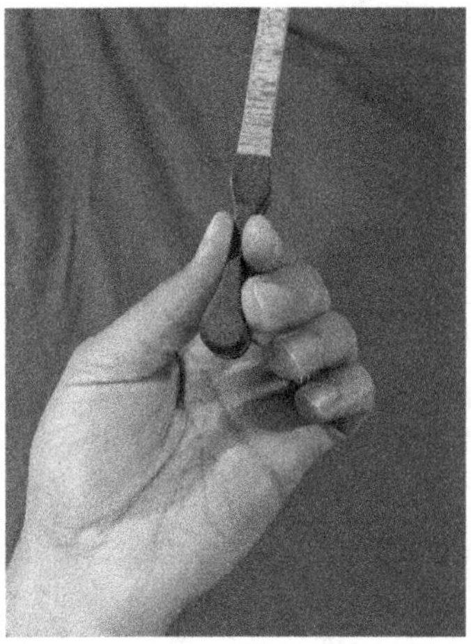
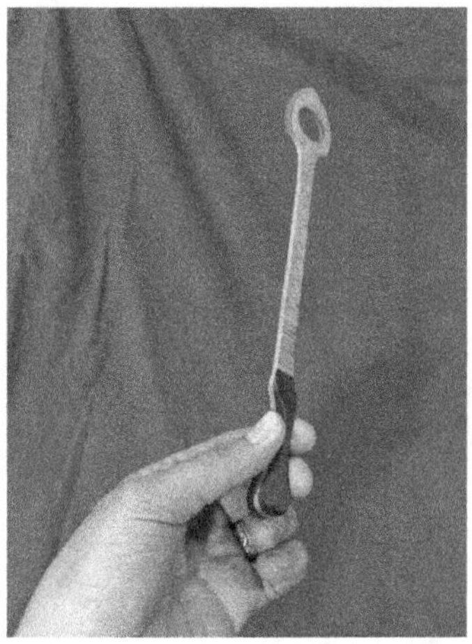
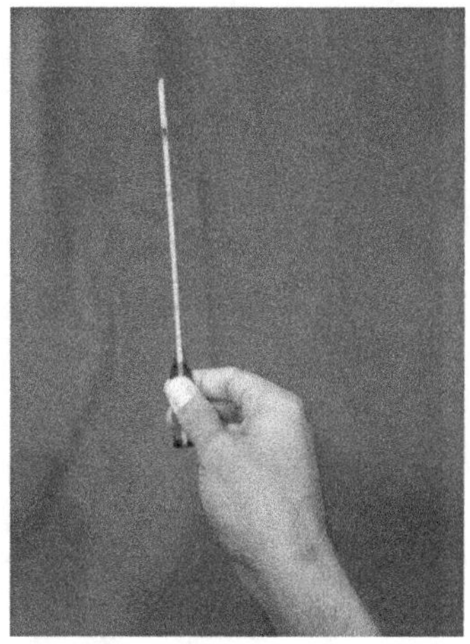
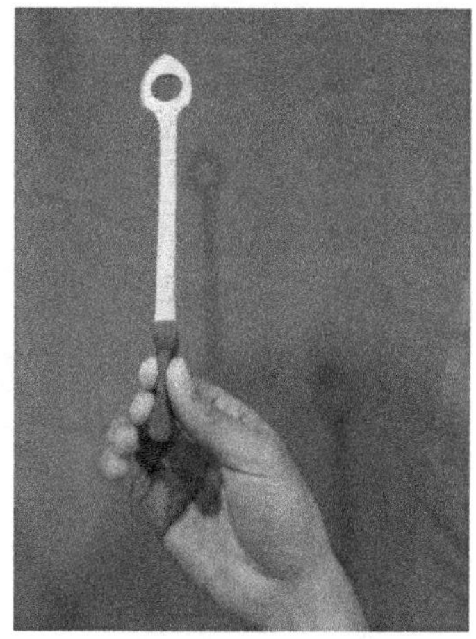

Passive Grip

Many great players use the passive grip successfully as their main grip. In my teaching and playing experience, this grip produces less accuracy and is less efficient. This is a "one-finger" grip as only the index finger is on the bottom and the thumb is on top. It is a passive hold because the motion originates in the elbow and pronation of the forearm rather than in the fingertips. The hammer subsequently flops as a result. I do use this grip when performing multiple bounce strokes and other rudiments because it facilitates the redirection of the rebound strokes.

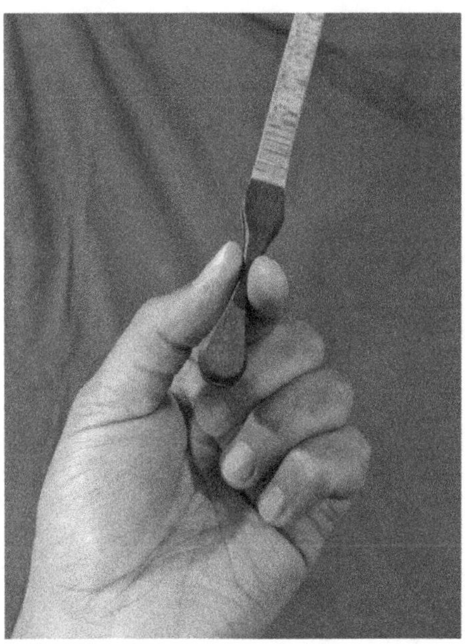
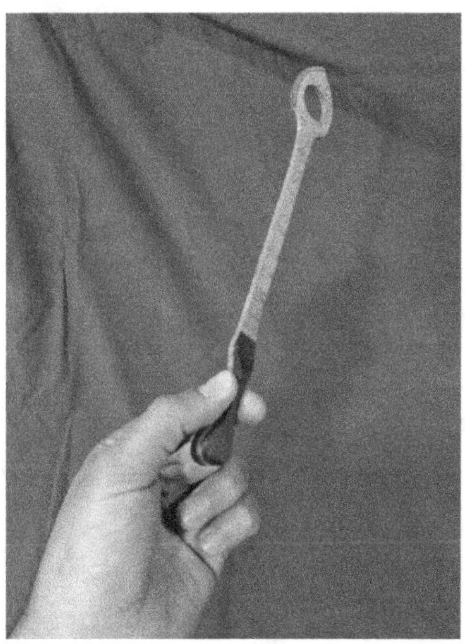
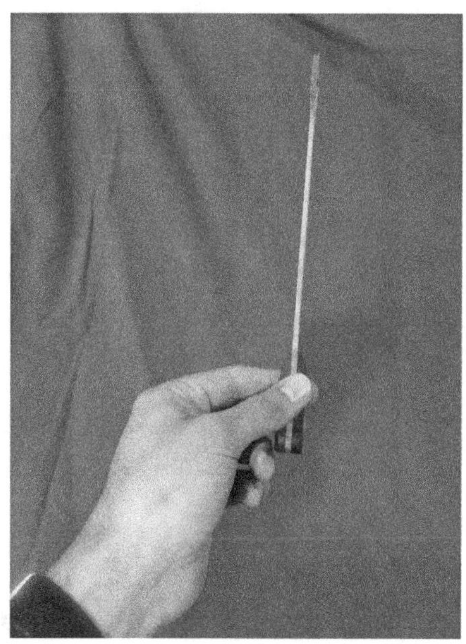

Hands!

The following exercises will improve your rhythm, accuracy and speed. Their simple patterns will also give you an opportunity to examine your hammer hold for optimum grip.

Duple Rhythm

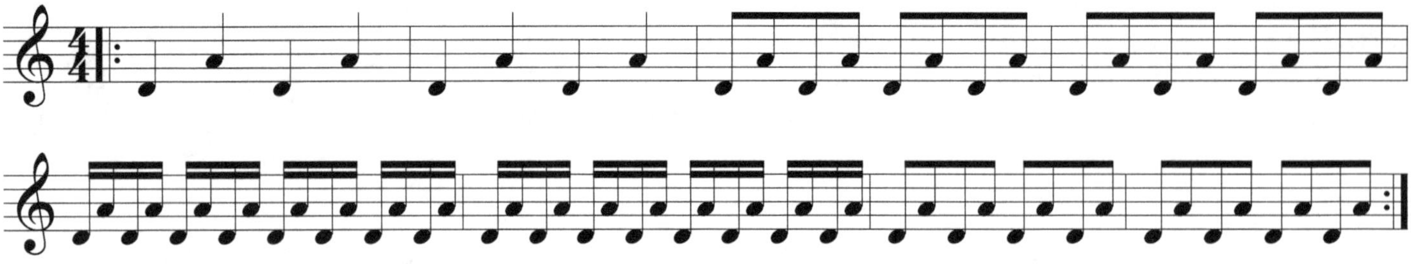

Triplet Rhythm

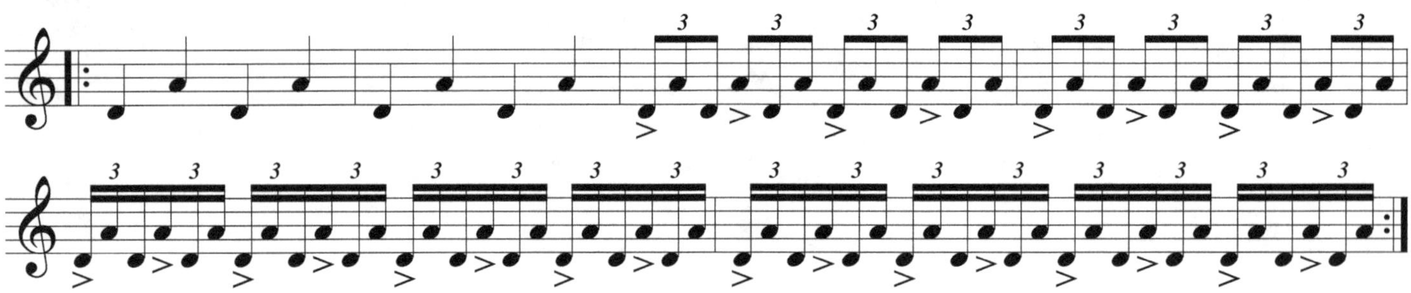

Left Pedal Points

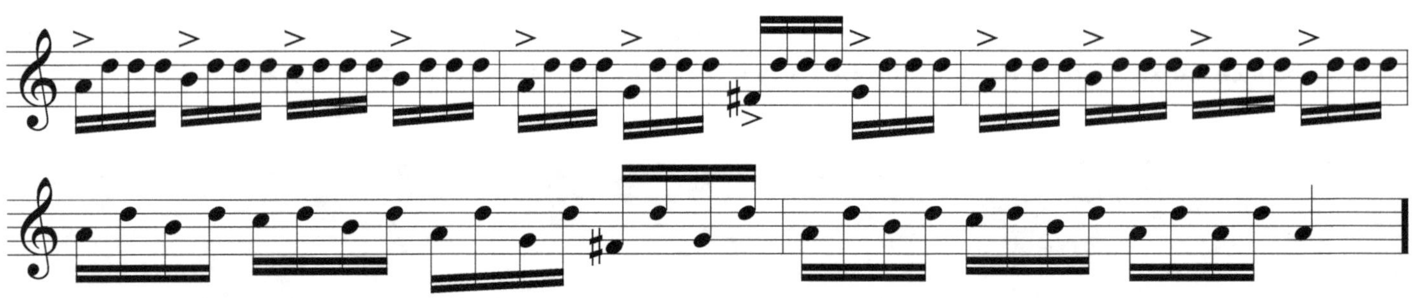

Right Pedal Points

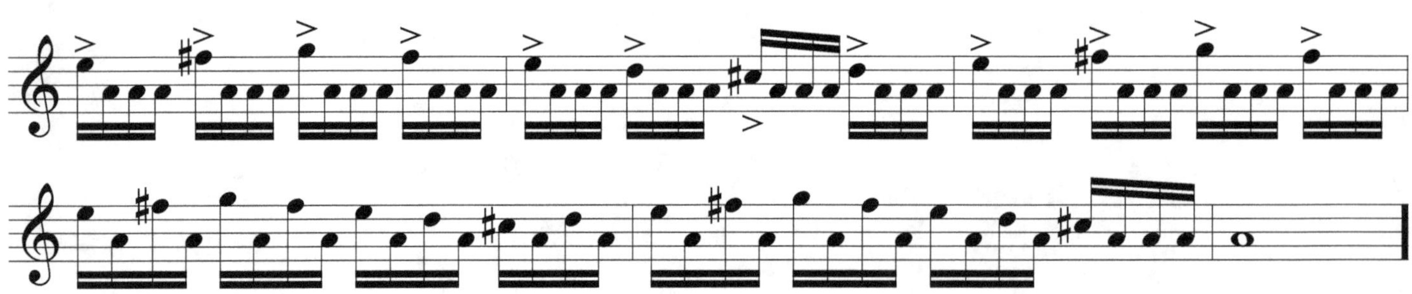

Octaves

Few exercises will align your hands and improve your aim like parallel octaves. Take these slowly at first and gradually build up your speed over time.

Treble Bridge

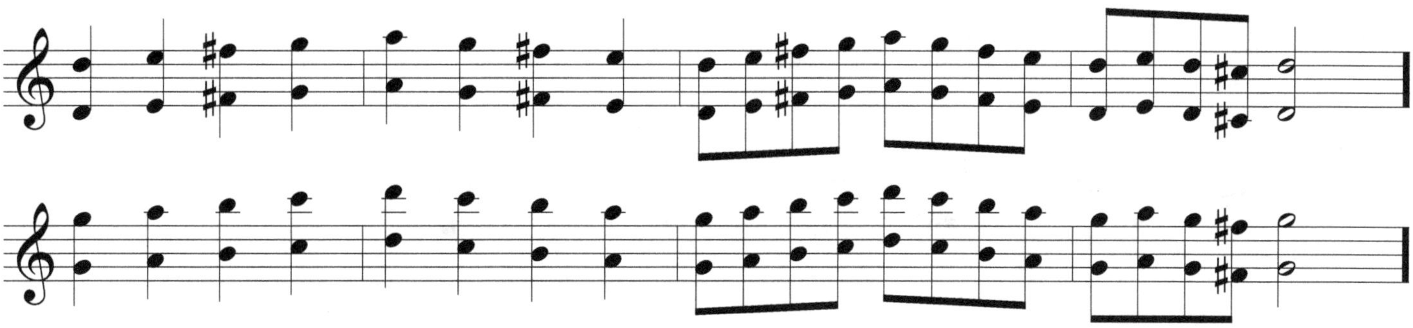

Bass Bridge

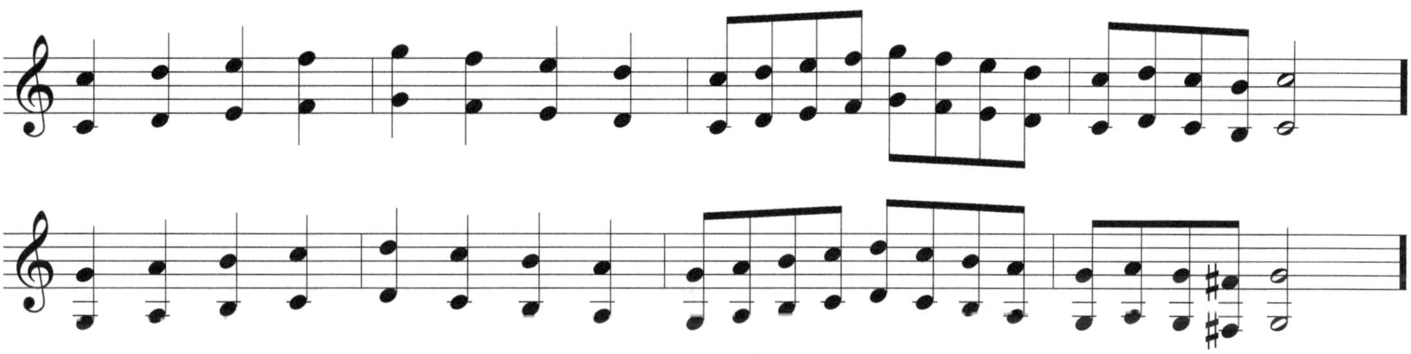

Displaced Octaves Starting with the Right Hand

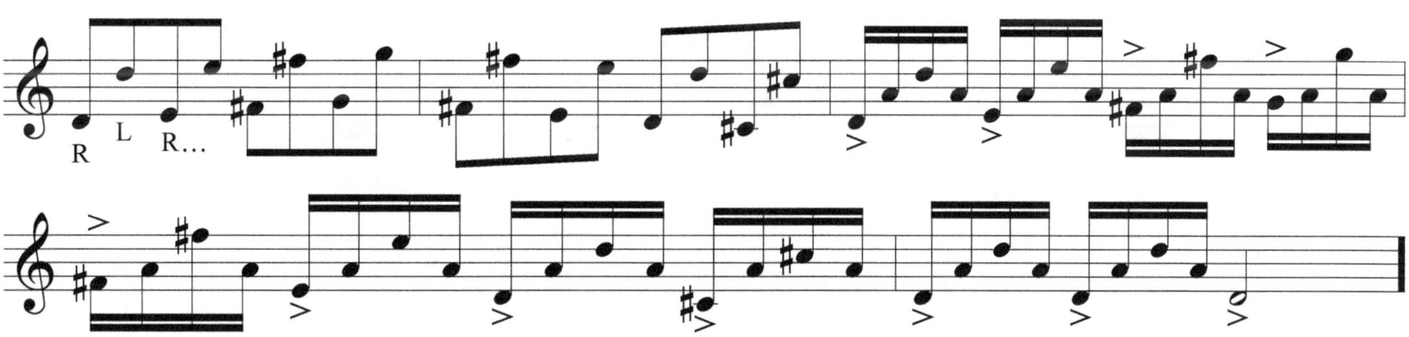

Displaced Octaves Starting with the Left Hand

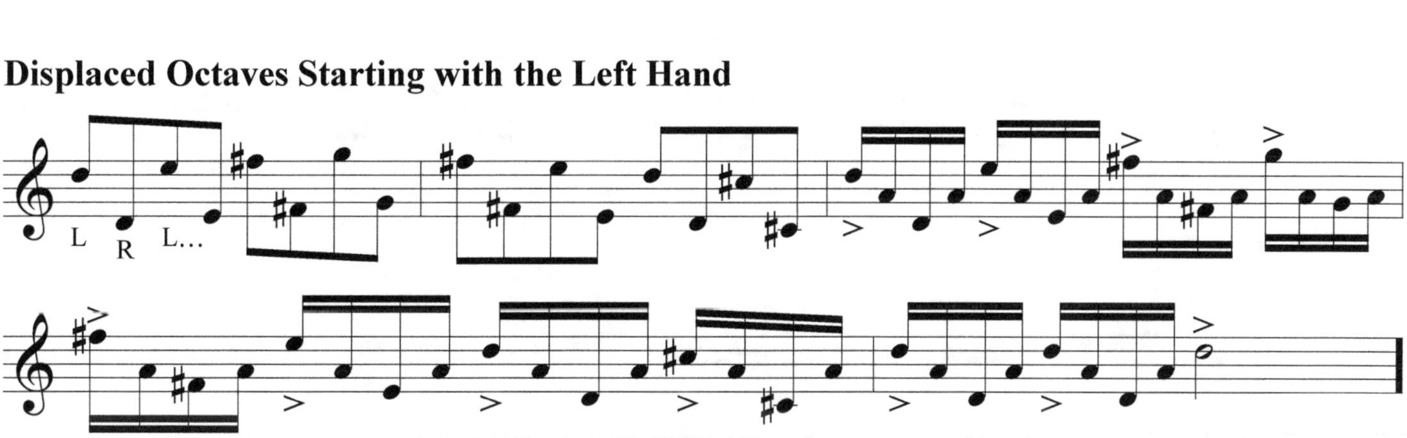

Flow!

If you can swat a mosquito when you feel a bite, your hands CAN move quickly! Everyone can! These exercises will help you build up speed and dexterity. Start slowly and listen to ensure that your non-dominant hand is not buzzing or rattling. I prefer to use dominant hand lead on these. While you are playing, scan your body for any tension. Relax your shoulders and neck to play these with the least amount of energy.

Bass Bridge Penta-Scales

G Major

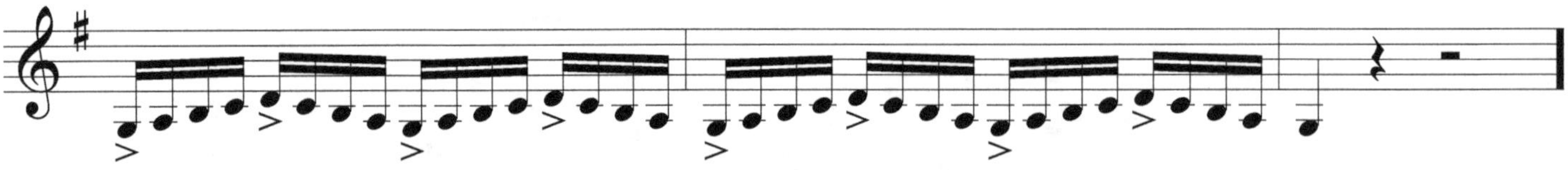

C Major

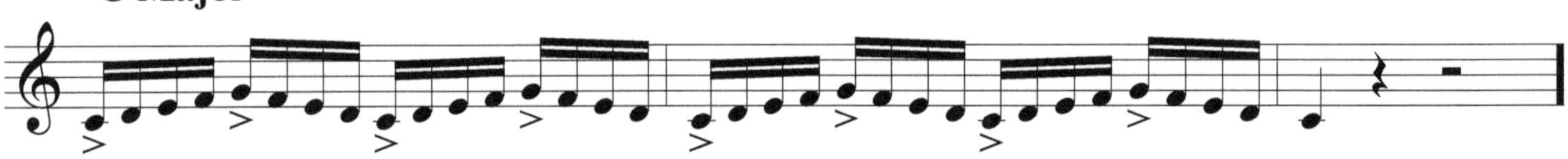

Right Treble Bridge Penta-Scales

D Major

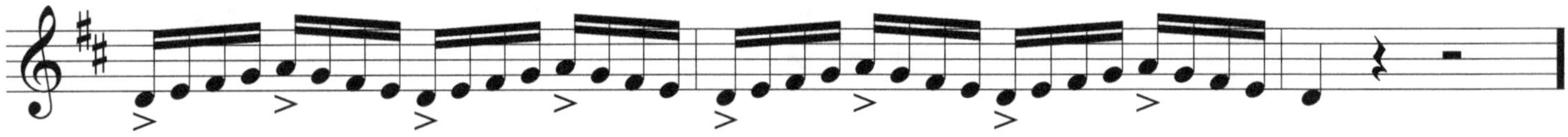

G Major

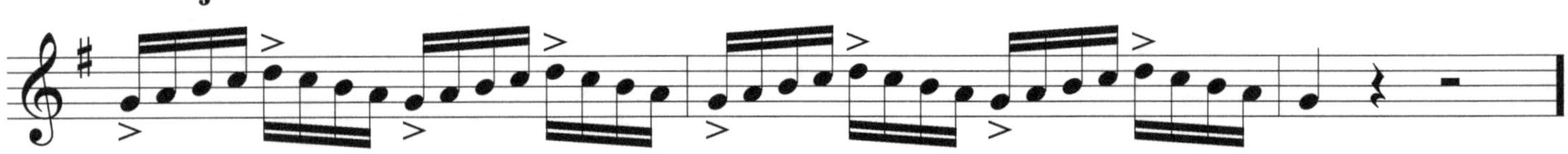

Left Treble Bridge Penta-Scales

A Major

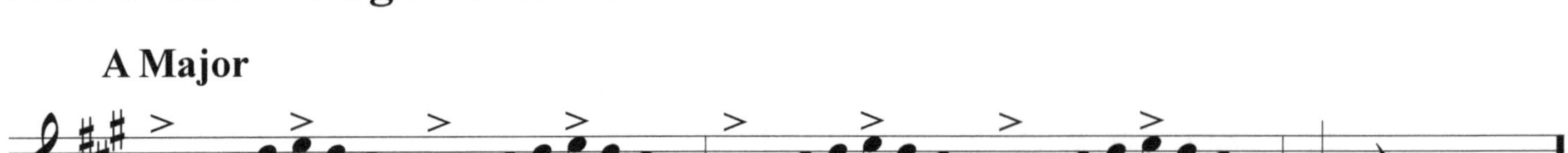

D Major

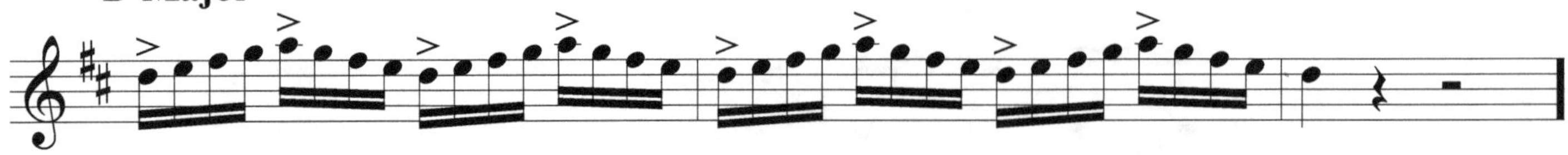

Rudiments

Rudiments are hammering and sticking patterns that evolved from formal percussion literature. Each unique skill was identified, labeled and listed in a series of rudiments for formal study and mastery. Most are so rhythm-specific that they do not directly translate well into melodic dulcimer playing. Nonetheless, master of all forty will most certainly improve your hammering—even if you do not perform them on the dulcimer.

I chose the following rudiments because they are immediately relevant to dulcimer playing or because they will directly improve a dulcimer skill. Their mastery will undoubtedly grant you *Killer Technique!* The following rudiments are useful in ornamenting melodies rhythmically and as unique articulations to the pitches, such as a ruff or a multiple bounce stroke. Spend a lot of time on this section if you struggle with rolls or with a non-dominant hand that unintentionally buzzes or doesn't spring up freely from the string.

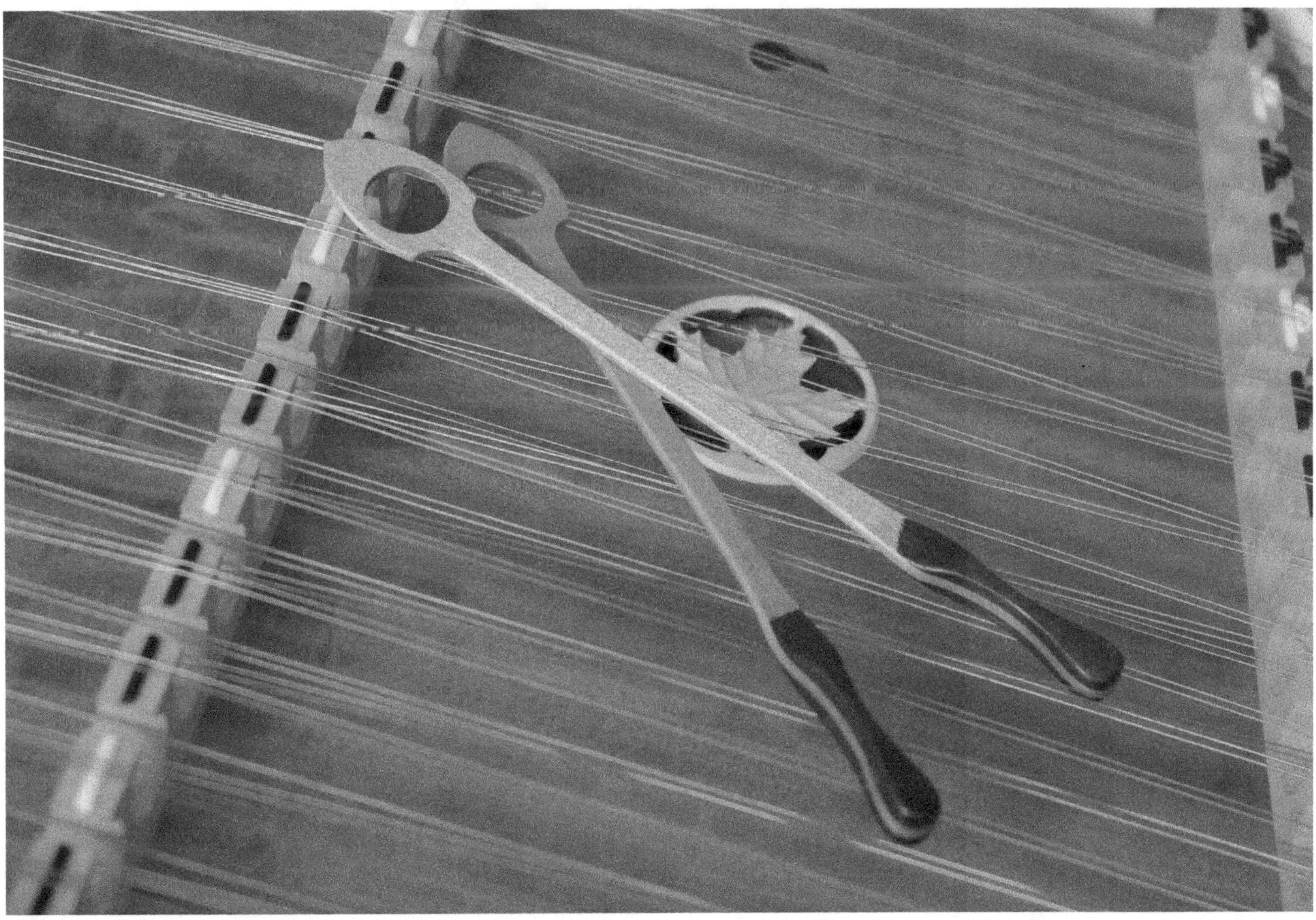

Multiple Bounce Roll

Multiple bounce rolls, also known as buzz rolls, are performed by allowing the hammer head to rebound back into the string. This results in an unmeasured "buzz" that often ornaments a note for emphasis. Mastering this rudiment requires the player to carefully balance the rebound force of the hammer head bouncing off the string against slight firmness needed in the thumb and finger of the grip to redirect the energy back into the string. Try to avoid buzzing a specific number of rebounds. The goal is a nice and tight buzz here.

1. Buzz Flops: Drop each hammer onto the string and try to get as many rebounds as possible with a relaxed grip.

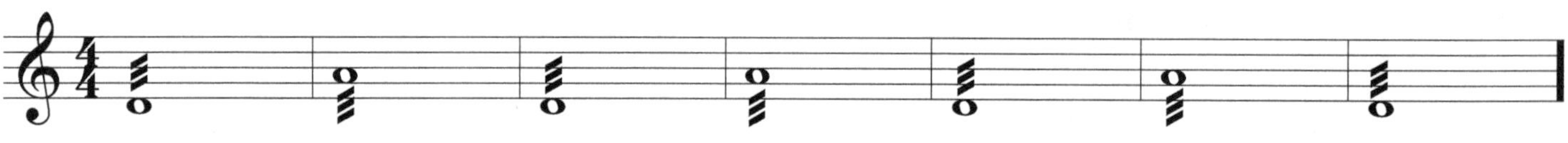

2. Connecting Buzzes: Now try to sustain each buzz until the next note to create a seamless buzz roll.

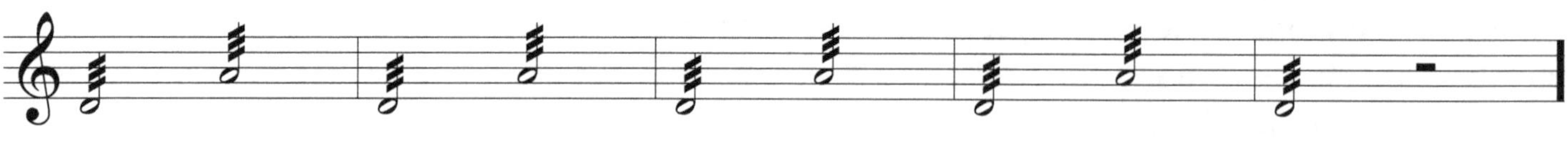

3. Tightening the Buzz: Same goal–connect each buzz into the next for a sustained roll.

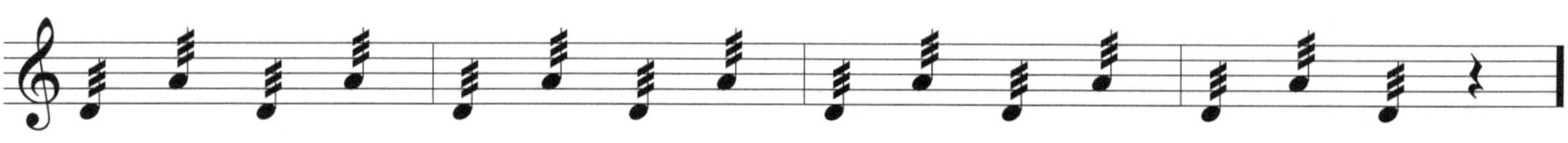

4. The Multiple Bounce Roll: The aim should be a roll with no pulse or lull.

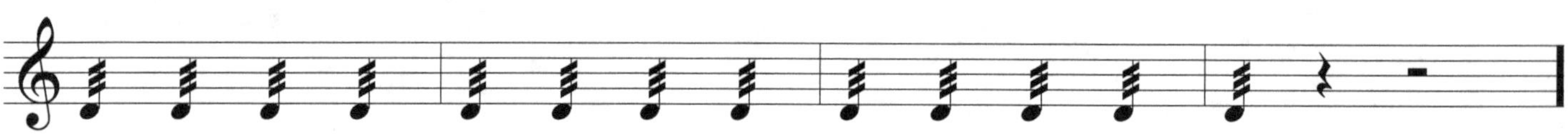

5. Buzzed Scales and Arpeggios: Treble D

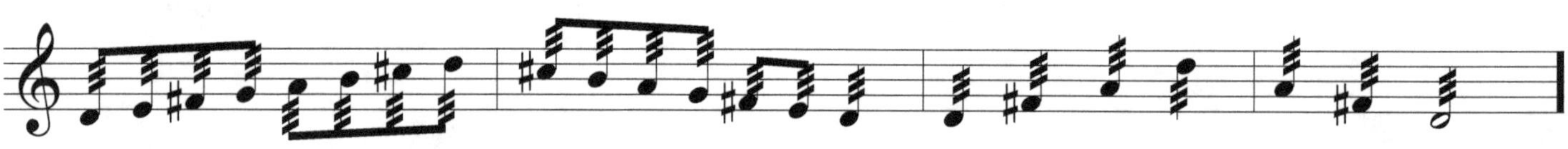

6. Treble G

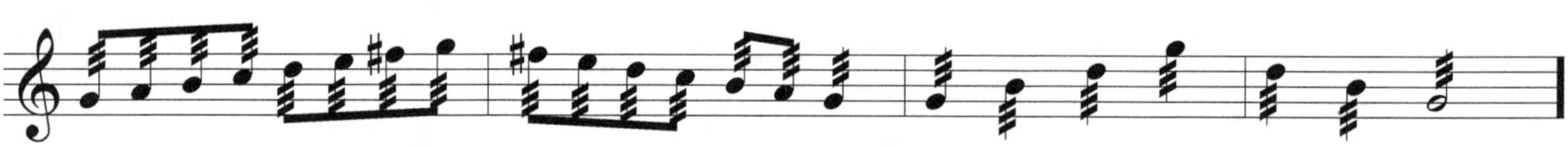

7. Buzzed Scales and Arpeggios: Bass G

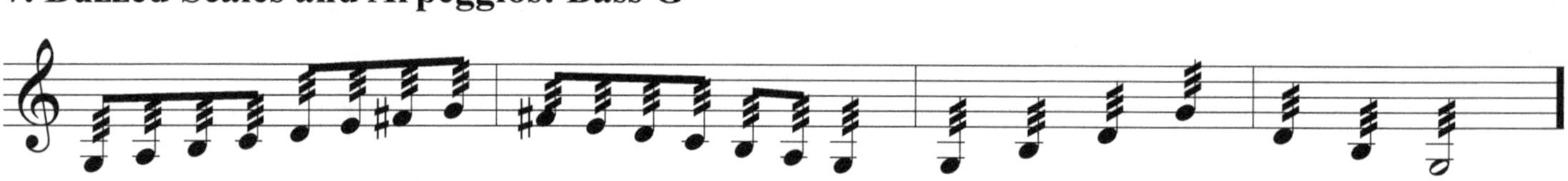

8. Bass Bridge Middle C

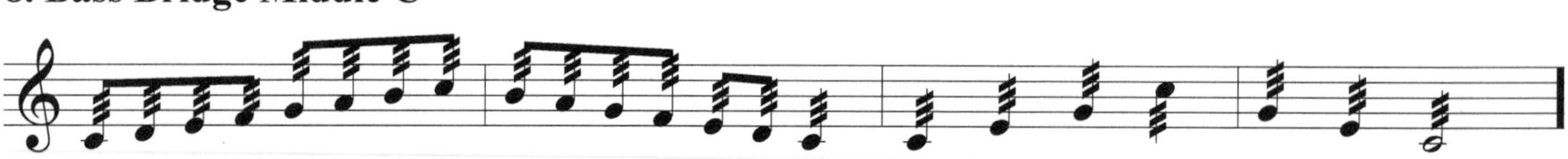

Triple Stroke Roll

This multiple bounce stroke is a controlled "roll" that consists of exactly 3 rebounds. All 3 notes of each triplet will occur with the same hand. The hand strikes only once and the 2nd and 3rd notes of each triplet group occur as rebound strikes.

1.

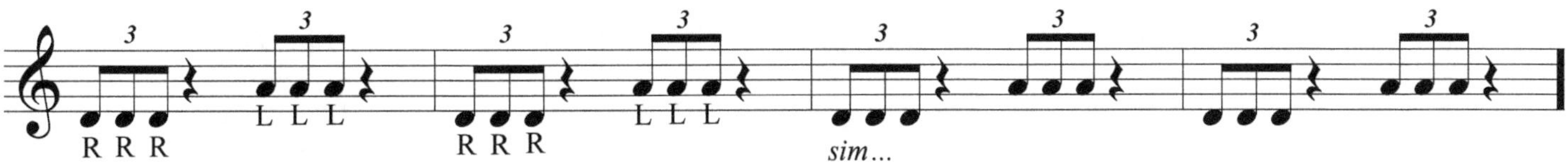

2.

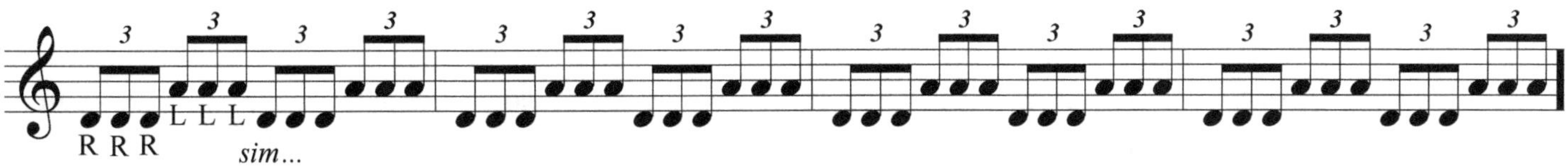

3. Triplet Stroke Roll Scale: Keep these smooth and even.

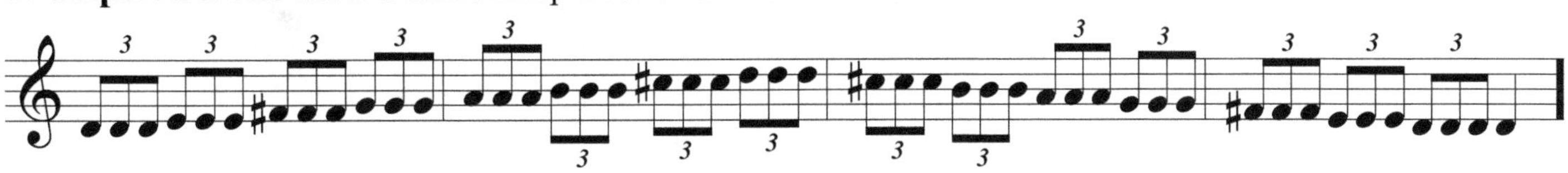

4. Skips: Start with either hand, but let the triplets come from multiple bounce strokes.

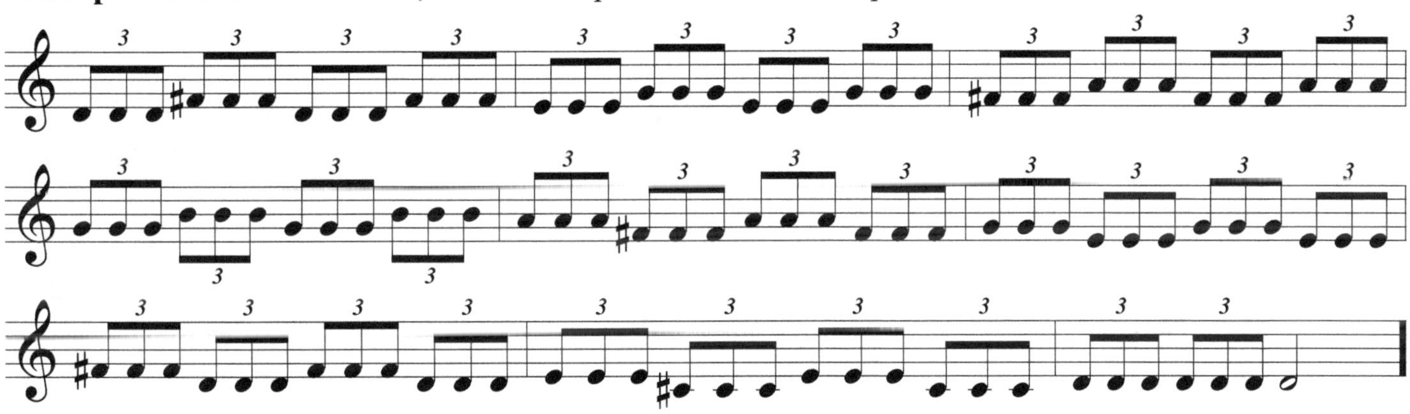

5. Across the Bridge

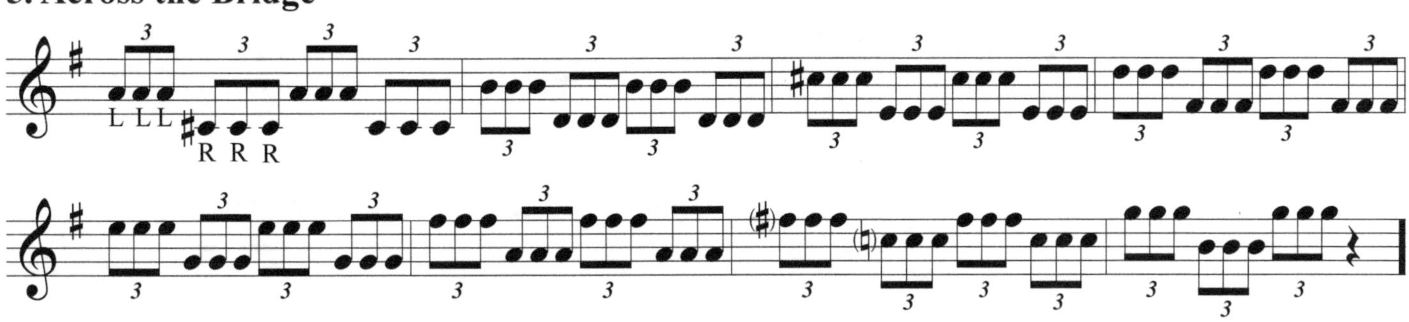

6. Cotton-Eyed Joe in Triplets

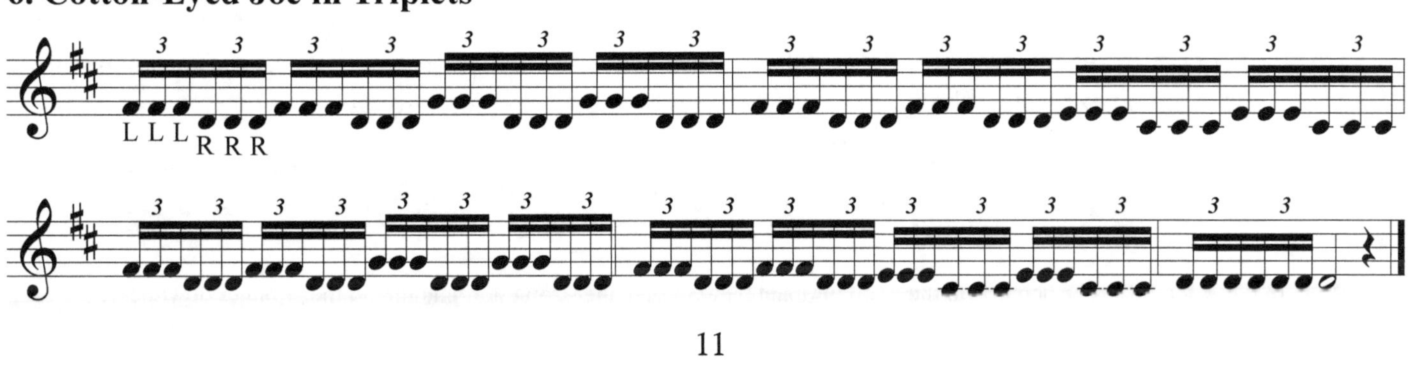

Double Stroke Open Roll

This rudiment is a series of double strokes in which the hammer is lifted after a second rebound stroke. Some players use this to embellish a simple melody by doubling every note quickly. Others use it to ornament individual notes for emphasis. Note the difference in notation here (2 slashes through the note stem versus three slashes used in a multiple bounce roll).

1. Mama / Papas: Strike once for the first eighth note and let the second hit come from the rebound.

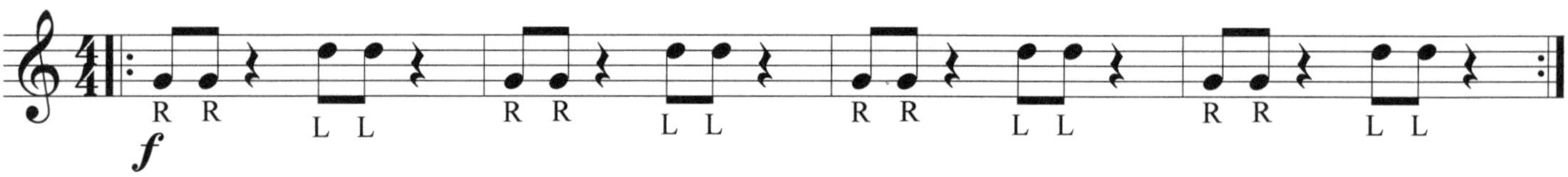

2. Seeing Double: Alternate hands in the first line–this is how you will strike the next line. In the second line, you will hit the 1st eighth note and allow the rebound to strike the 2nd for each pair.

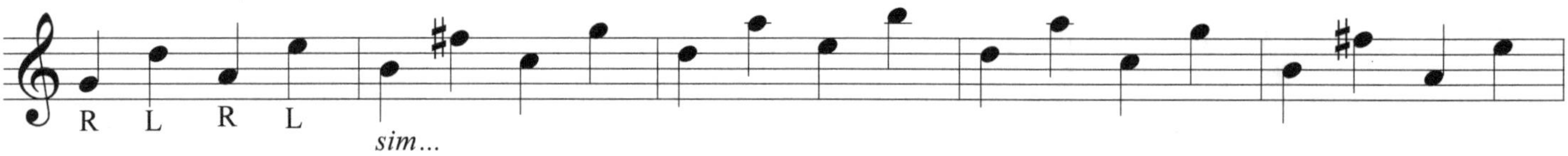

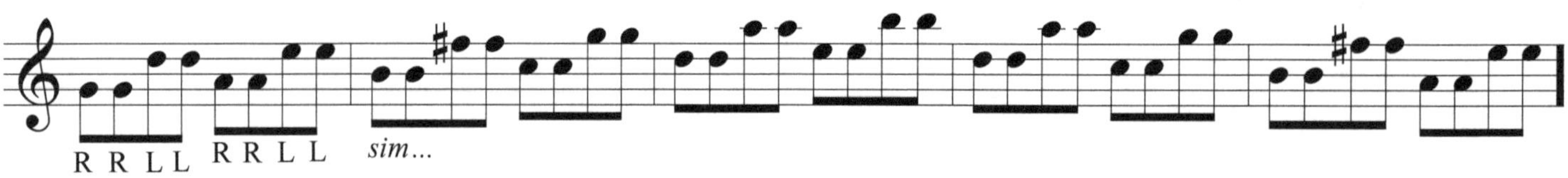

3. Giddy Up! Hit once for the 1st 16th note, double bounce for the 2nd, and use your left hand for the 8th notes. Notice that your hands will actually only strike twice on each string as the 2nd 16th note is a bounce rather than its own strike.

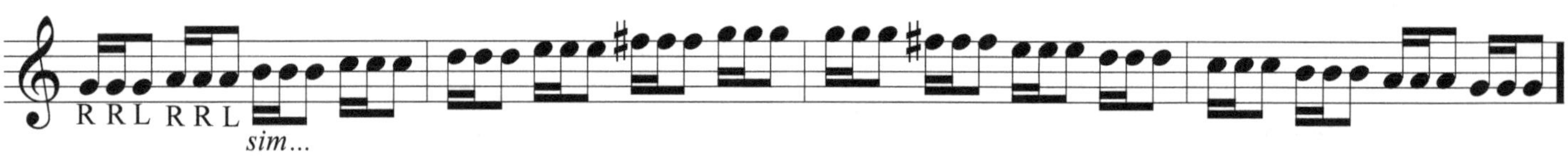

4. Run Horsey! This is similar to the exercise above except now the double stroke will fall on your left hand.

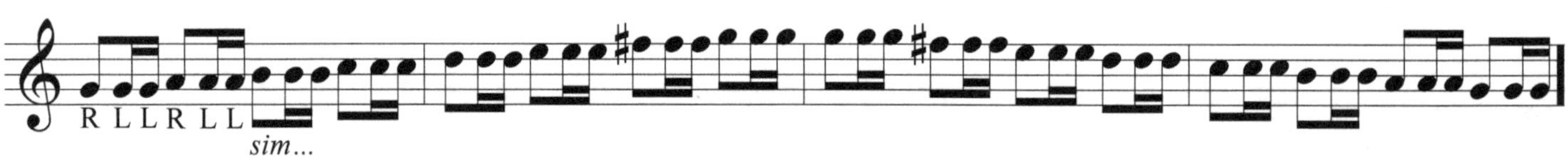

5. Double Stroke Rolls are also notated like this. It still means to double bounce each 8th note.

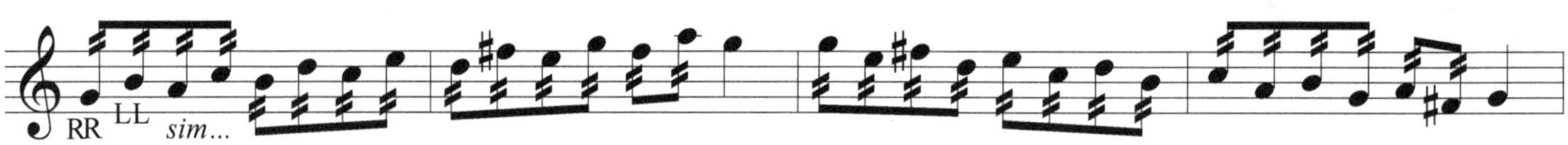

6. Application: Also notated as grace notes, the double strokes in this excerpt from *Scotland the Brave* are a good example of how they can ornament melodies rhythmically.

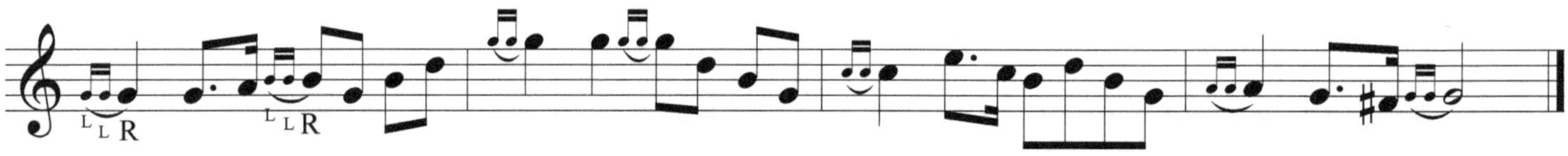

Note that the double stroke happens in the non-dominant hand to give the strong dominant hand the stronger downbeats.

Five Stroke Roll

This rudiment is great for developing stick control even though it does not have a lot of practical application on its own. It is an especially good measure of how even your control is between your right and left hands. In short, if you can do this well, you will have *Killer Technique* to apply to all of your playing!

1. Warm-Ups: These are just two double bounce strokes ended with a single tap–left & right handed.

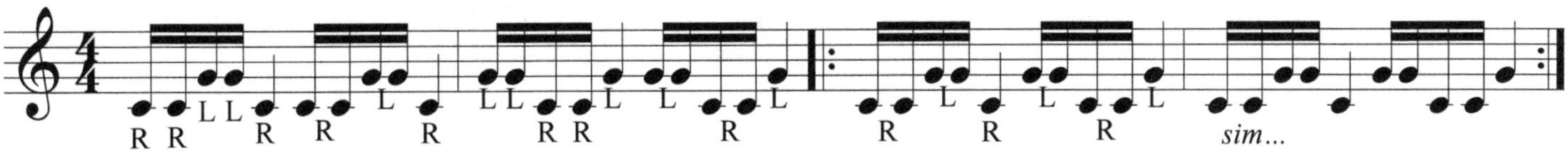

Notation:

What it sounds like: What your hands do: How it is written:

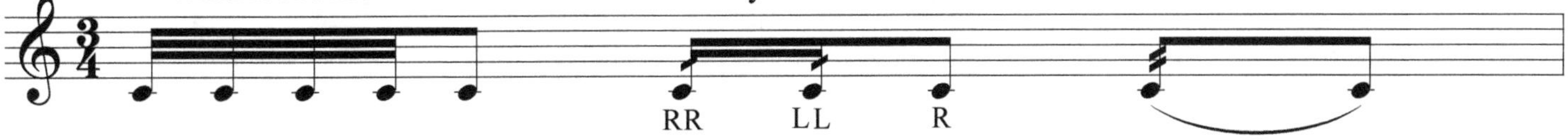

2. Base Stroke: This is what your hands will hit before you try the double bouncing. This is the base stroke.

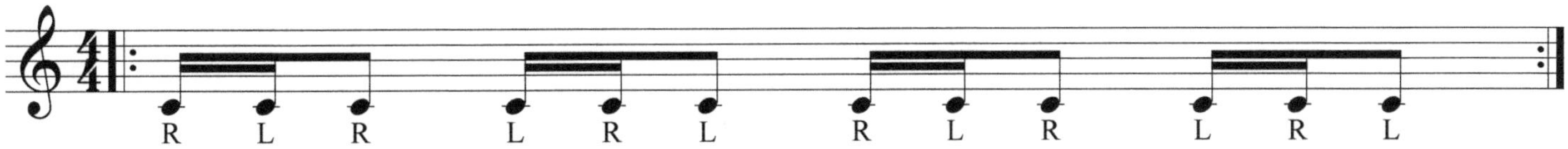

3. Getting Started: Now adding the double bounces to the base stroke, this is the 5-Stroke Roll. The second measure here shows the standard notation for this rudiment.

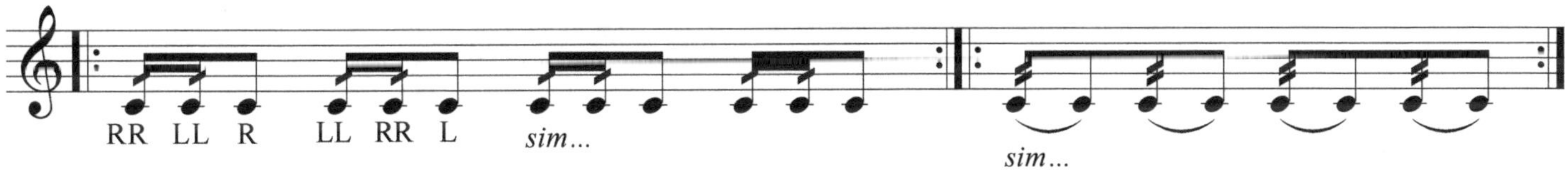

Paradiddles

Paradiddles are also an excellent way to achieve equal dexterity and control between your hands.

1.

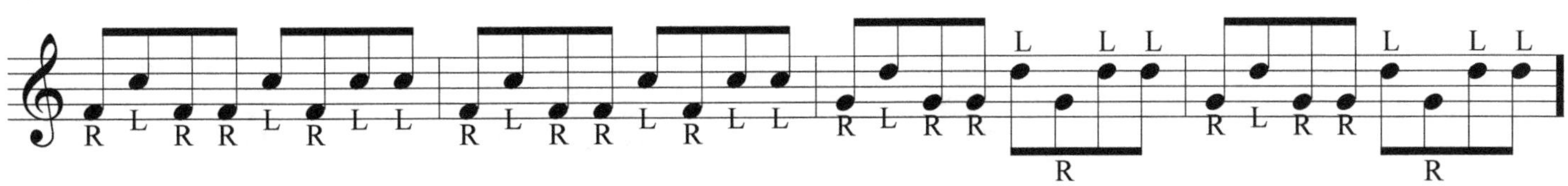

2. Paradiddle Groove

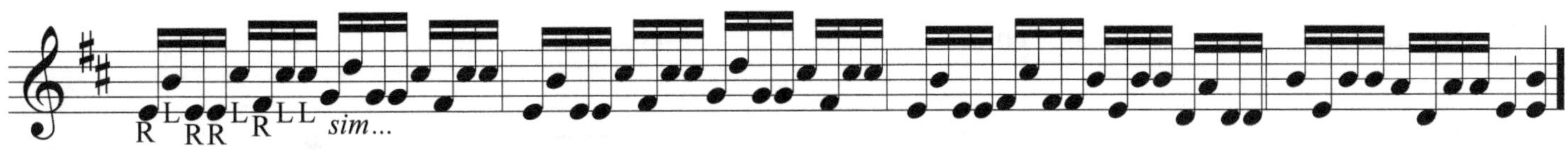

3. Paradiddle Scale: Try all scales beginning with both right and left hands.

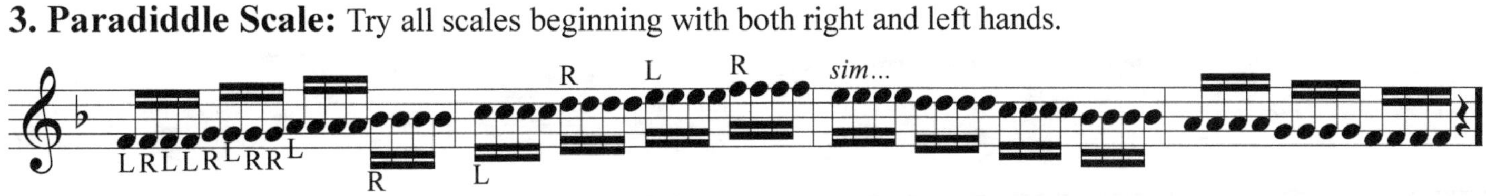

Flam

Flams are a common way to rhythmically embellish a melody. Typically the flam ornaments strong beats for emphasis. This technique is performed by dropping the hammers from different heights. The primary note will sound louder because it is dropped from a greater height with more velocity. The grace note will be softer and will hit just before the primary note because it starts closer to the string. The space between the two can vary.

1. Ffl-lams: This rudiment sounds just like it's name–"ffl" (the grace note) "lam" (the primary note).

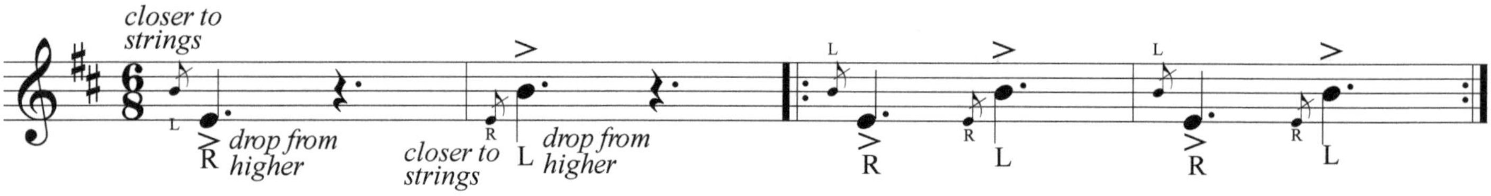

2. Right and Left Flams

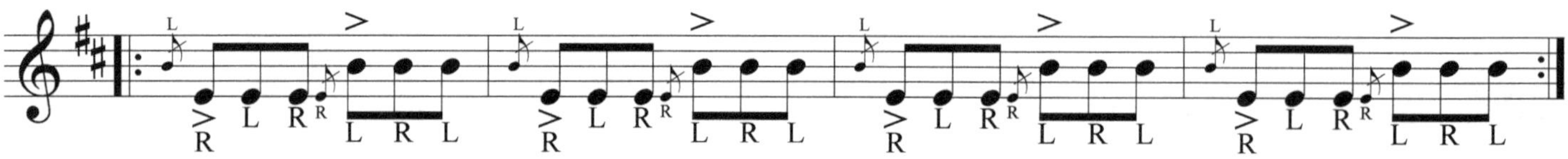

3. Duple Meter Flams

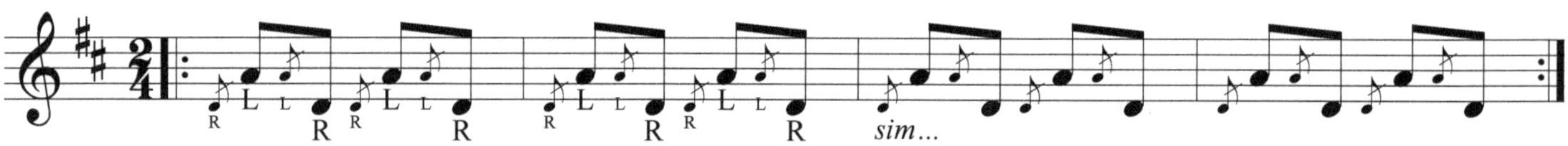

4. Flams to Go

To the Left **To the Right**

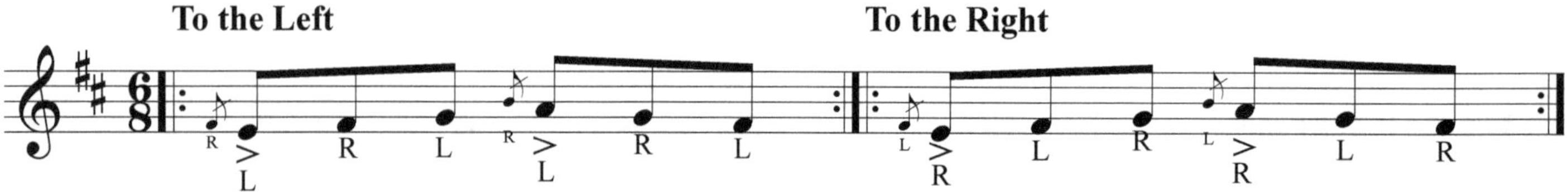

Dorian Scale

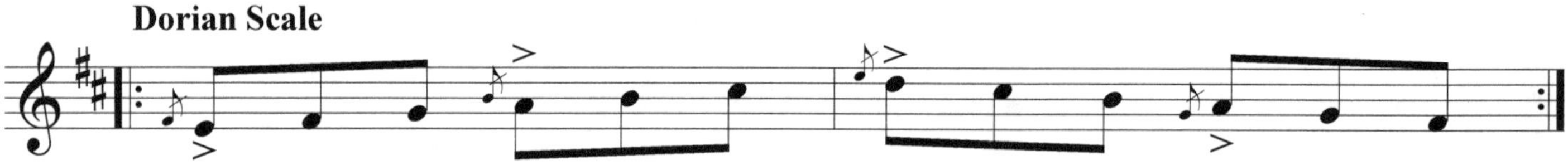

5. Application: Morrison's Jig. This excerpt shows how this rudiment can ornament a melody line.

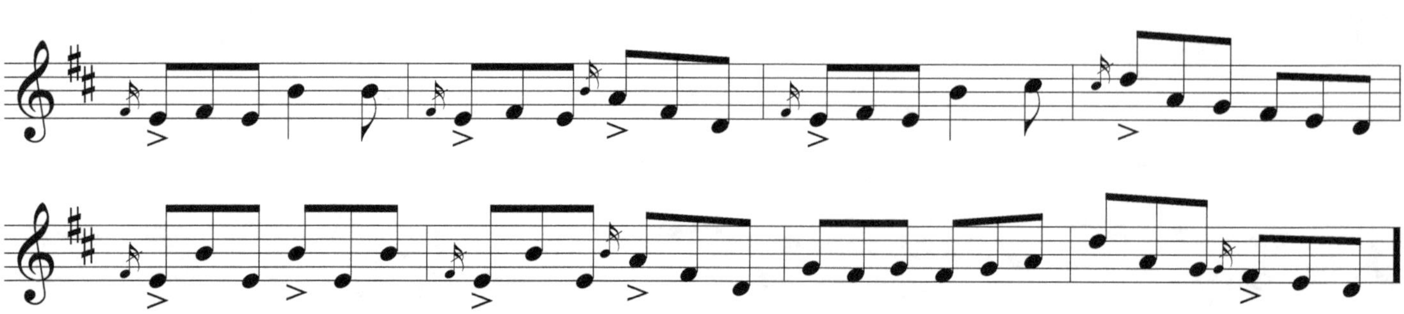

Drag (Ruff)

A drag, or ruff, is important to have in your technique arsenal. It is a good barometer of efficient hammer facility and a commonly used embellishment. In particular, this rudiment helps to fill leaps when chording. It is similar to a flam in execution, but consists of a double bounce instead of a single bounce. The hand for the primary note will drop from a higher starting position.

1. The Drag

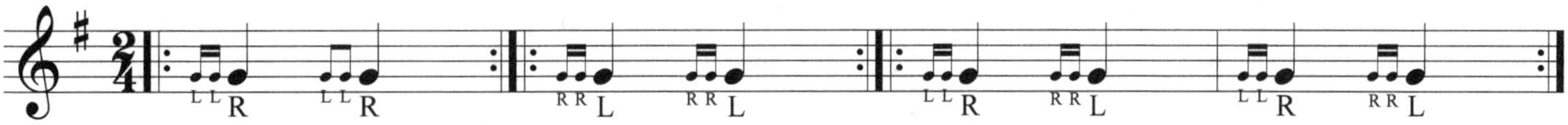

2. Ruff Times

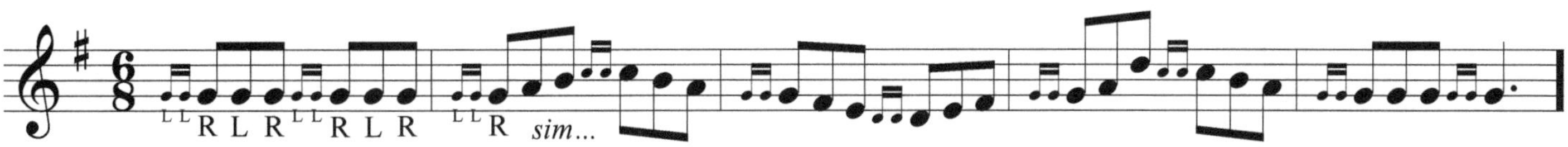

3. Across the Valley: This is a drag that many right-handed players use because the drag occurs on the right hand. Notice that the right hand double bounce stroke will first hit the right treble bridge note and rebound onto the bass bridge note. As a result, the melody will fall on the left hand. Be certain that both right hand notes in the drag are double bounce strokes rather than separate strikes.

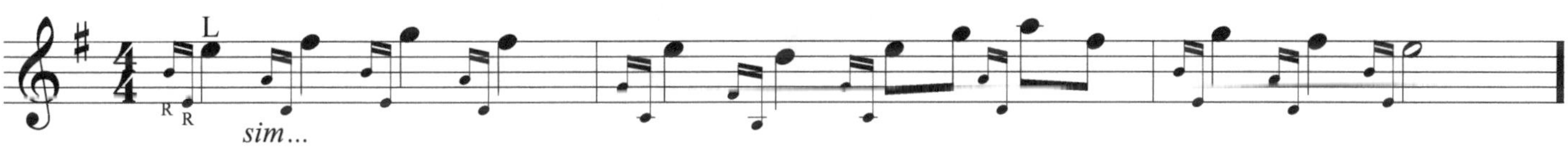

4. Ruffing Up 6ths: Here is another common way we utilize the drag. These are almost all begun with drags a 6th below (on the right side) the melody. Tip: When multiple chord tones are written simultaneously, as in the last measure, always roll from the bottom up.

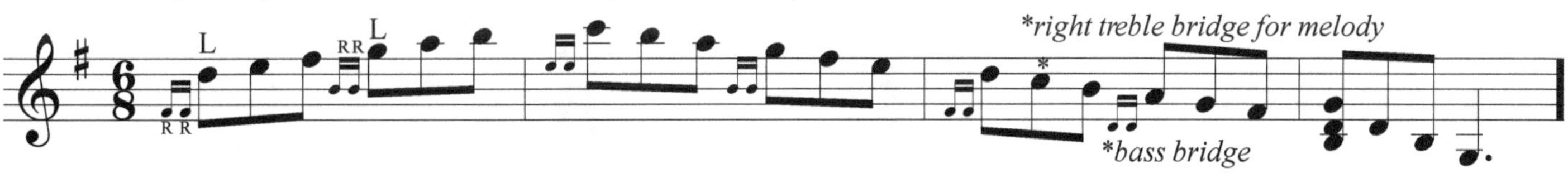

5. Application: ***Minuet in G*, J.S. Bach**

This excerpt demonstrates how the drag can smooth wide harmonic leaps. Tip: All the notes with stems that point down will be played with the right hand. I play this with all the drags on the bass bridge with my right hand.

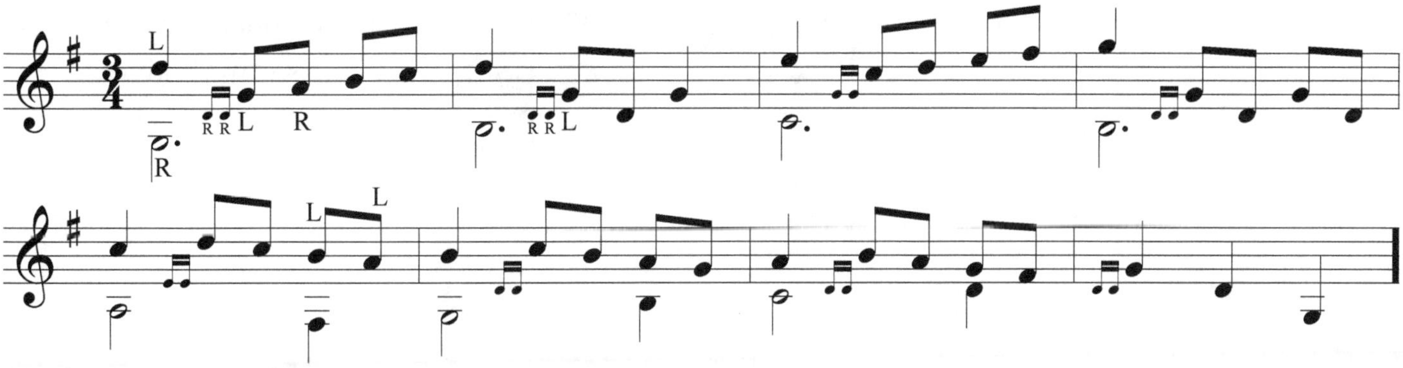

Patterns

To achieve *Killer Technique*, you must have common patterns under your hands without thinking about them. In addition to scales, it is important to know chords, arpeggios and chord suffixes. There are several ways to render chords on the dulcimer. Below are the most common. When beginning on a bridge marker, they are called "First Position;" when begun one above a marker, they are called "Second Position." The most commonly used are 1st Position Major and 2nd Position Minor. Use the guides below to find these patterns for the following exercises. The use of rhythms and meters to displace accents in these exercises is a clever trick to acquire muscle memory faster.

First Position Major:

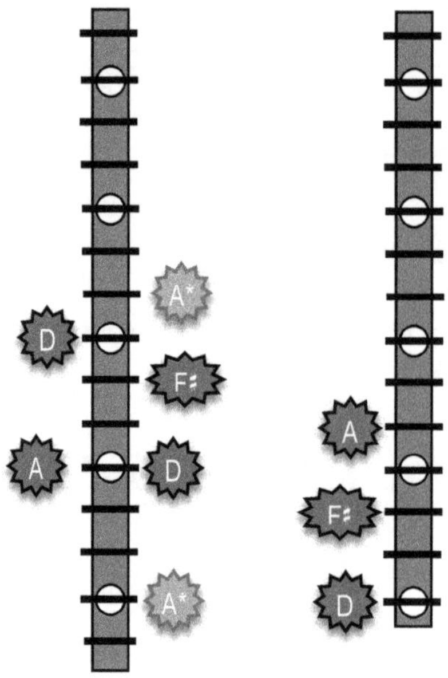

Example: D Major
The darker pattern is for right-handed players. The lighter "A*"s are for left-handed players. This chart shows both octaves.

Second Position Minor:

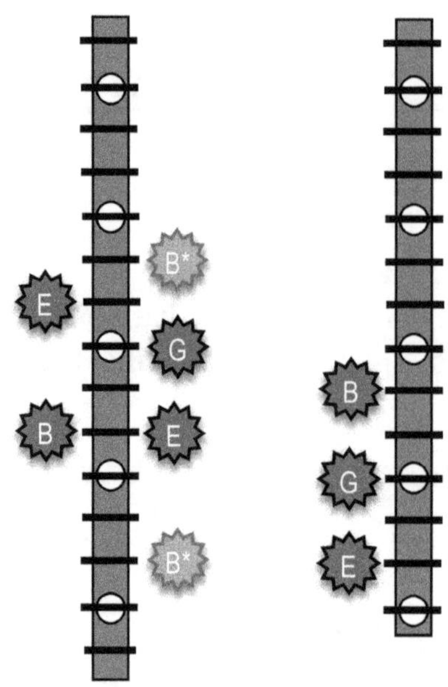

Example: E minor
The darker pattern is for right-handed players. The lighter "B*"s are for left-handed players. This chart shows both octaves.

Arpeggios:

From the Italian word "Arpa" (harp), an arpeggio is a harp-like rendering of a chord wherein each note is played in succession rather than at once like a piano. There are right- and left-handed versions of all of these but you should be familiar with both patterns.

1. 1st Position Major Arpeggios: 1 Octave

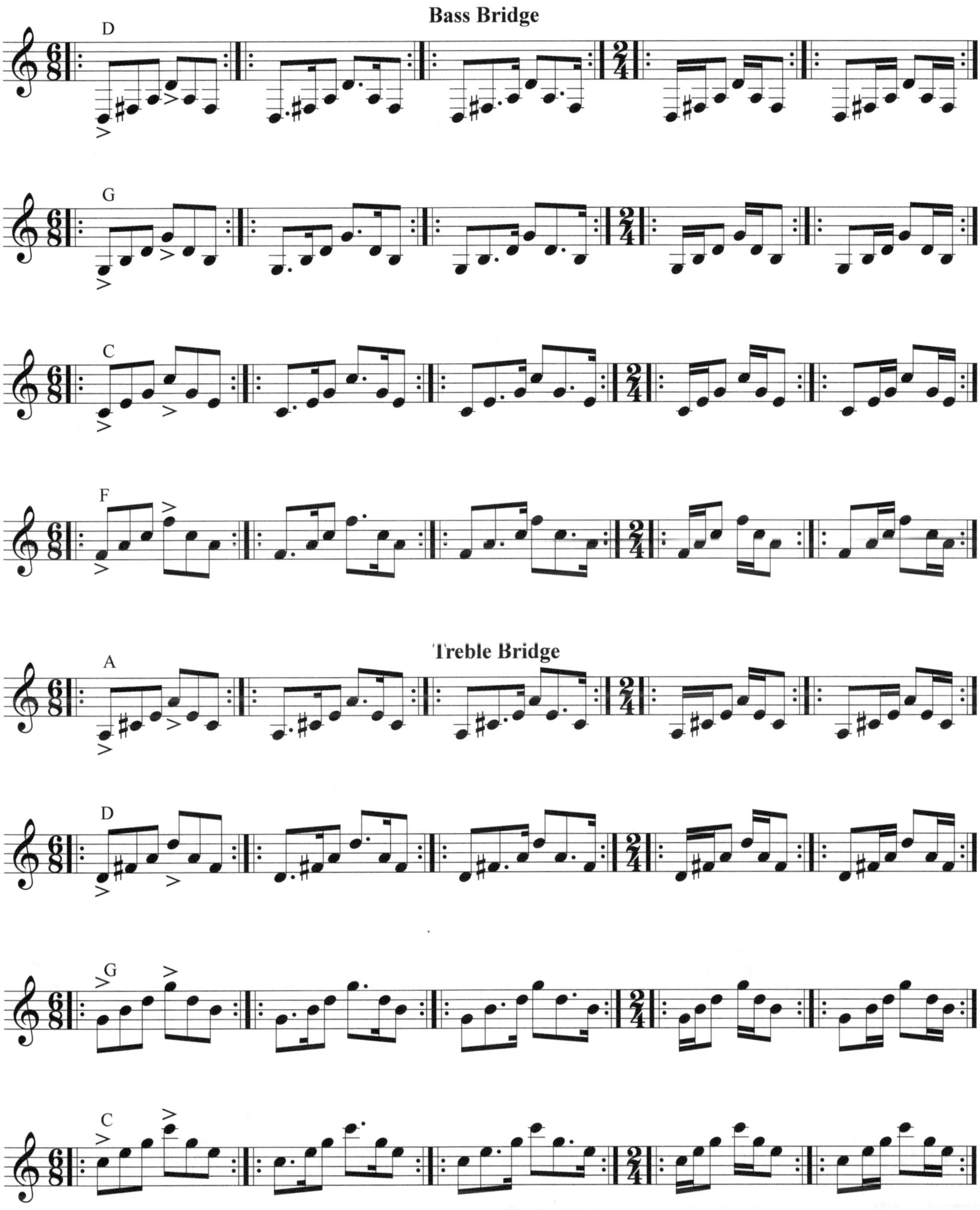

2. 2nd Position Minor Arpeggios: 1 Octave

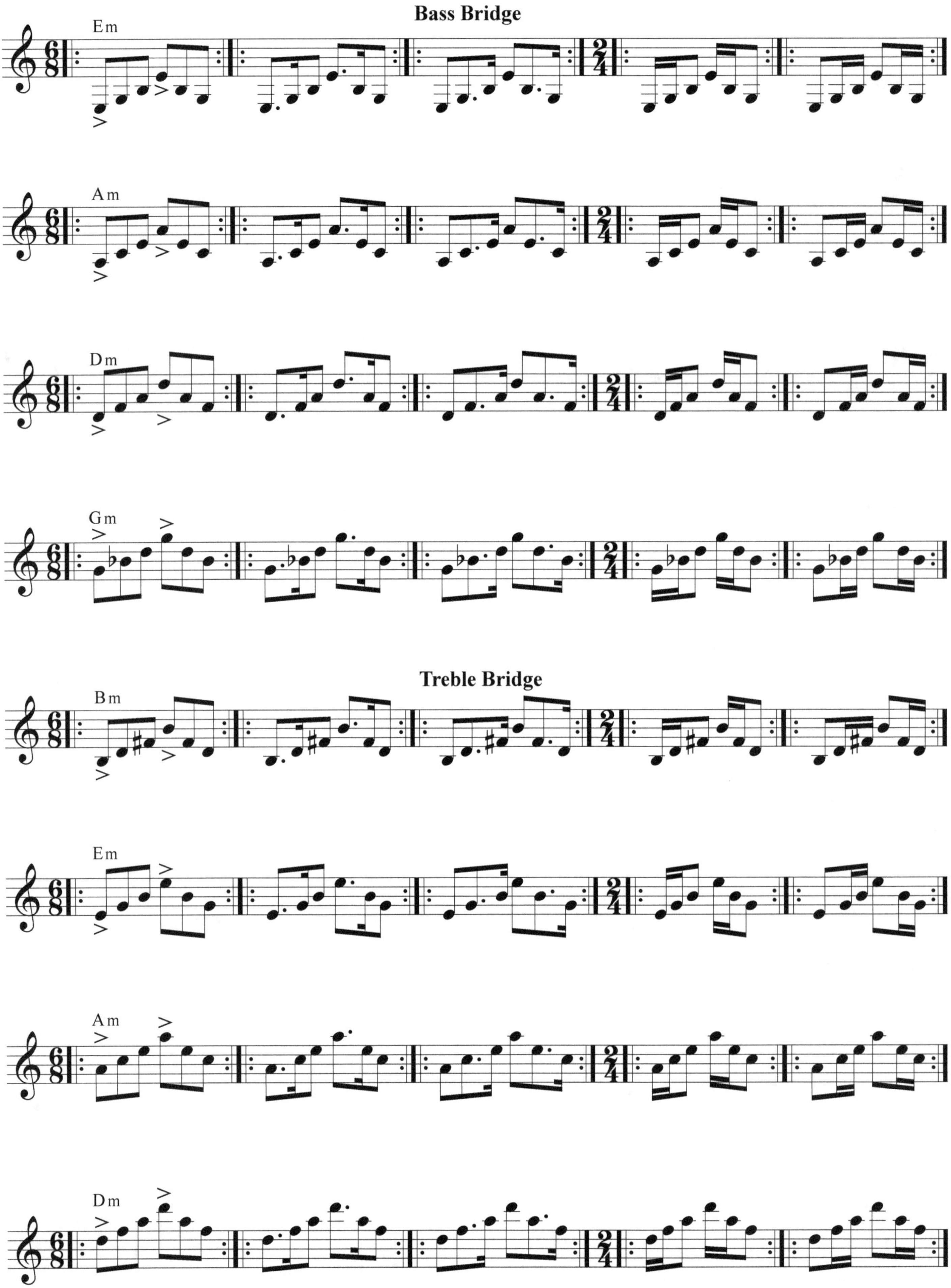

3. 1st Position Major Arpeggios: 2 Octaves

D Major

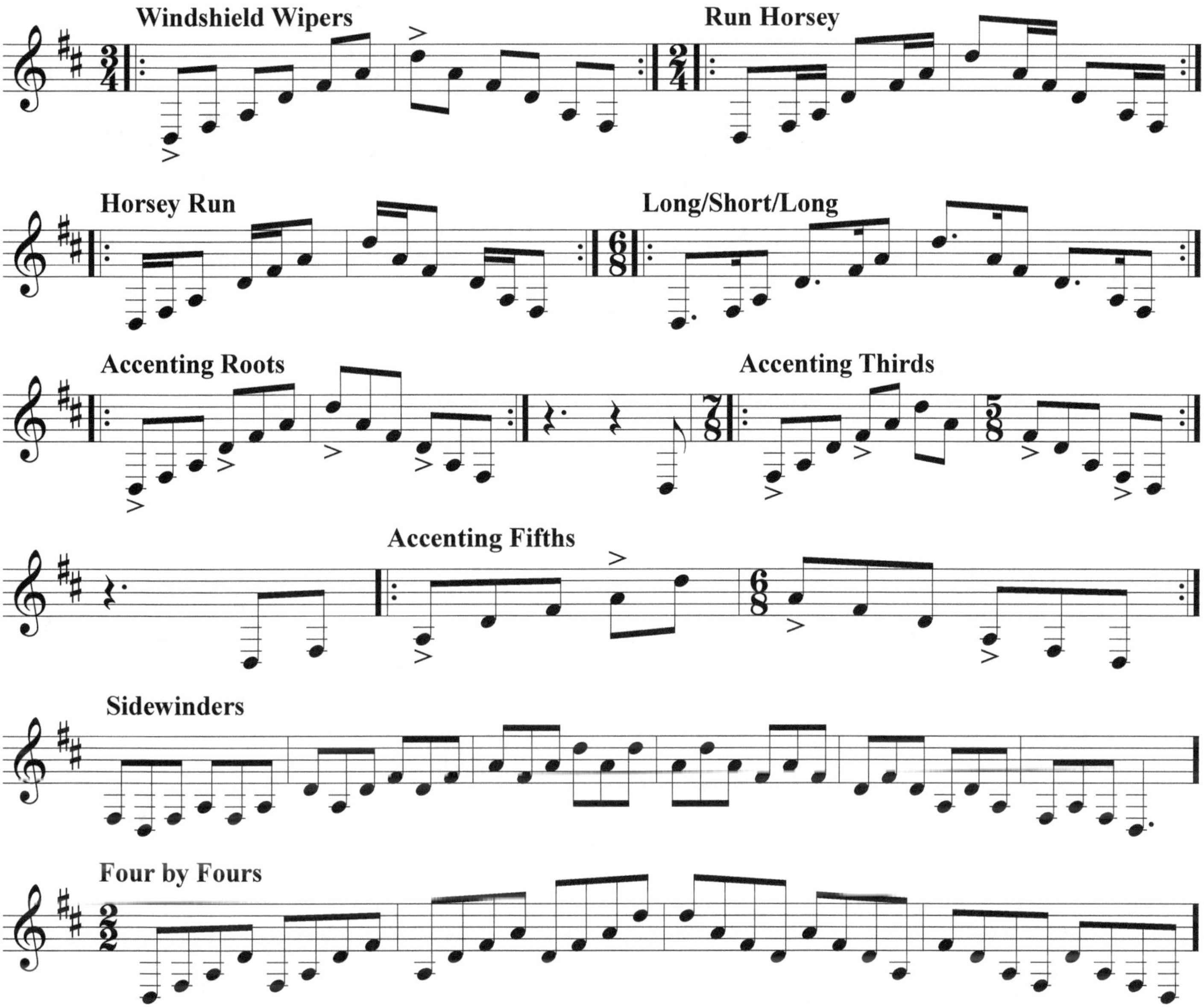

G Major

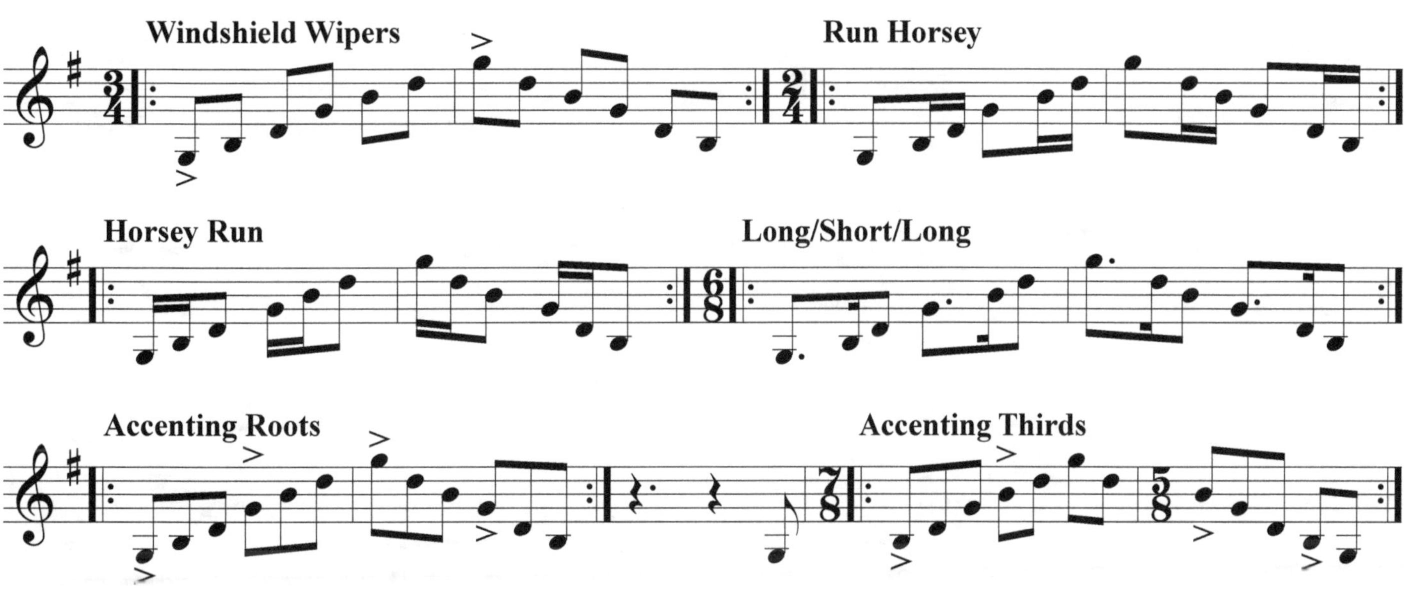

Accenting Fifths

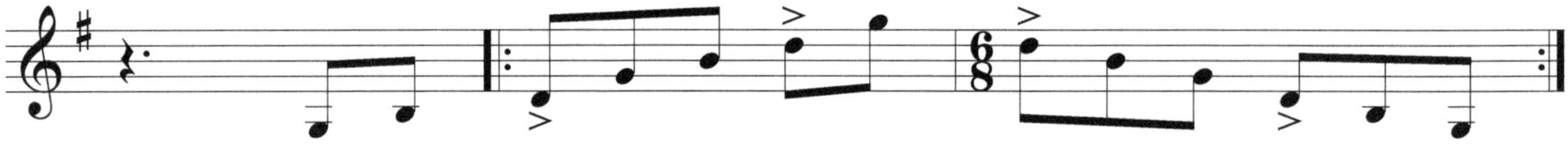

Sidewinders

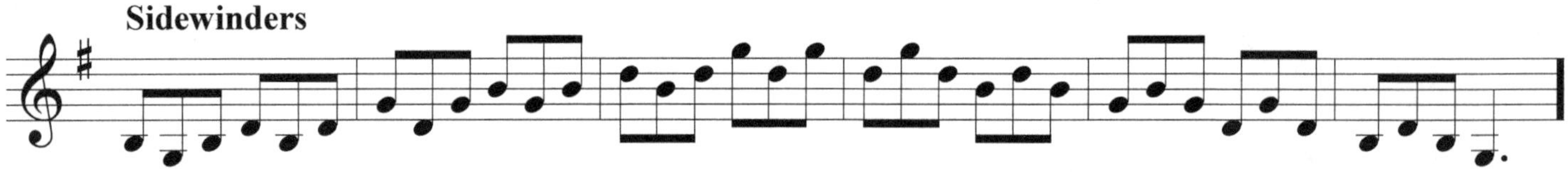

Four by Fours

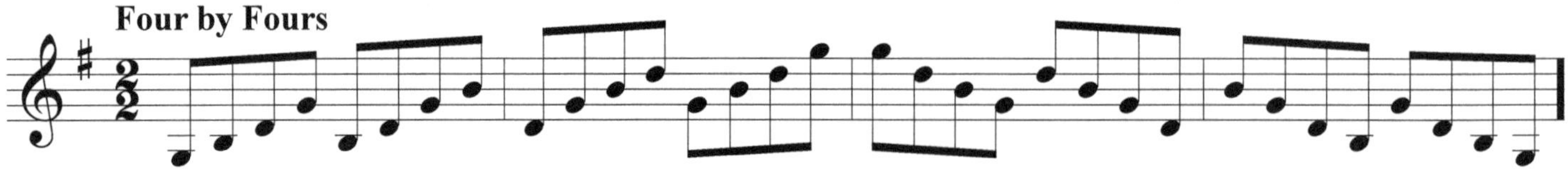

C Major

Windshield Wipers — Run Horsey

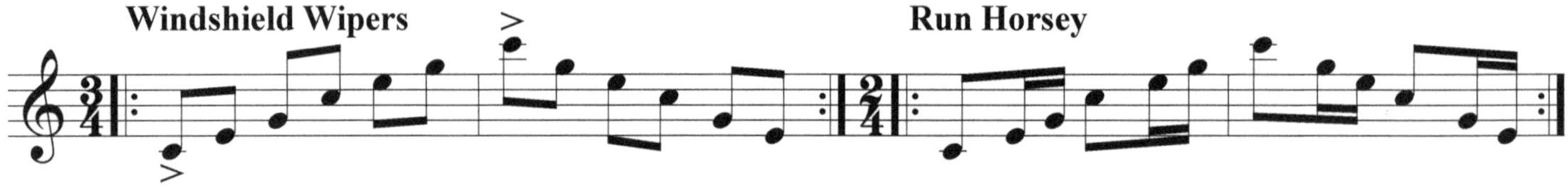

Horsey Run — Long/Short/Long

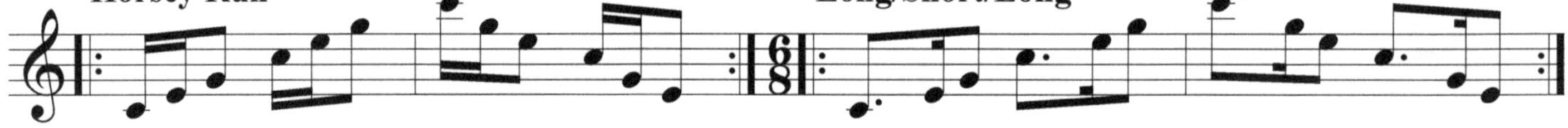

Accenting Roots — Accenting Thirds

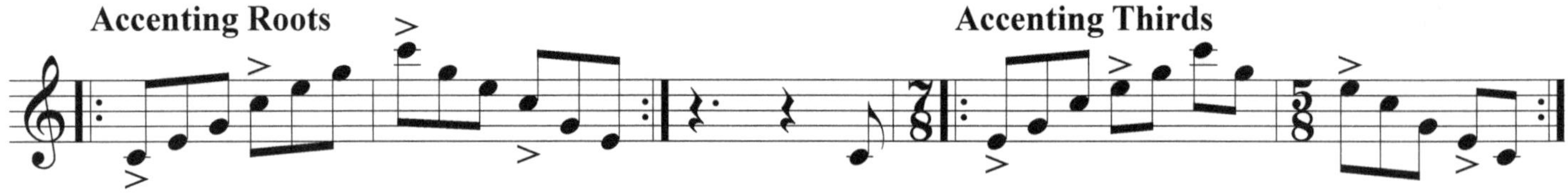

Accenting Fifths

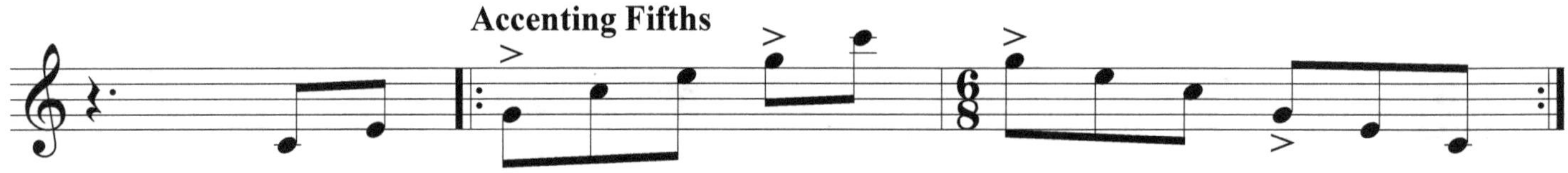

Sidewinders

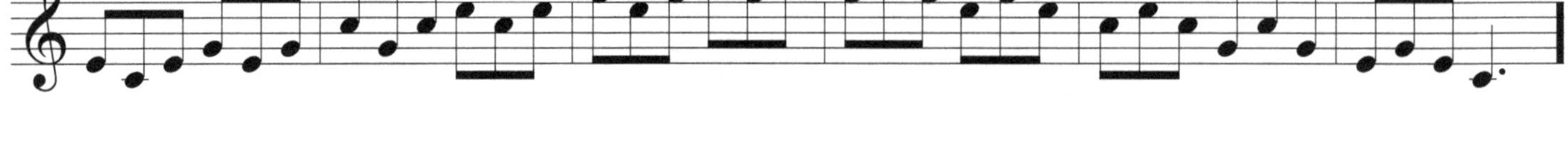

Four by Fours

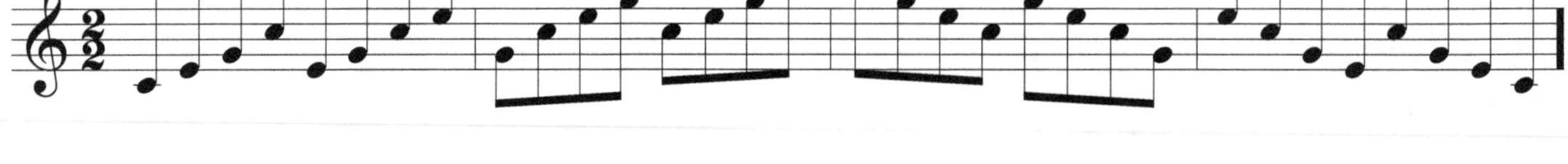

2nd Position Minor Arpeggios: 2 Octaves

E Minor

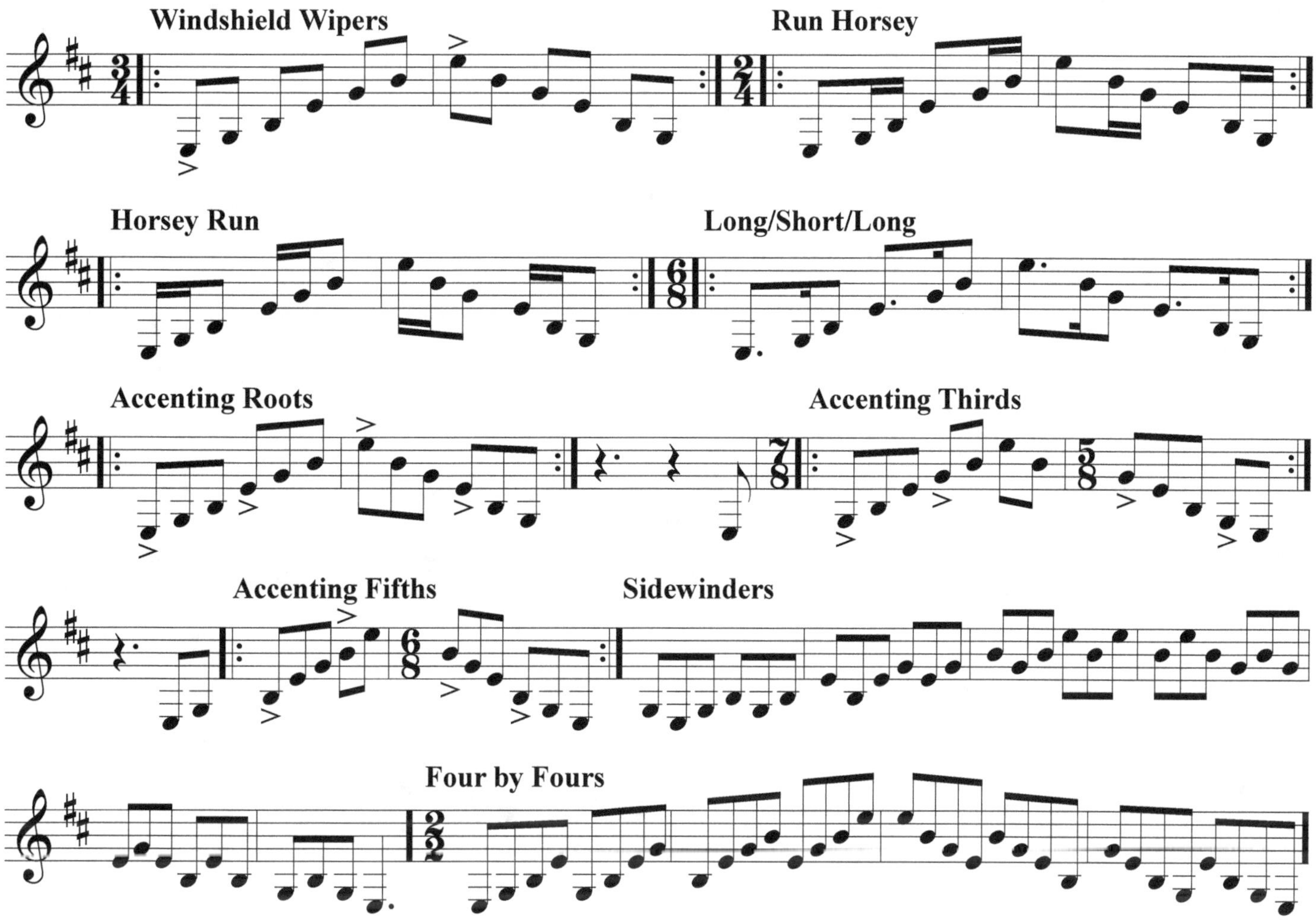

A Minor

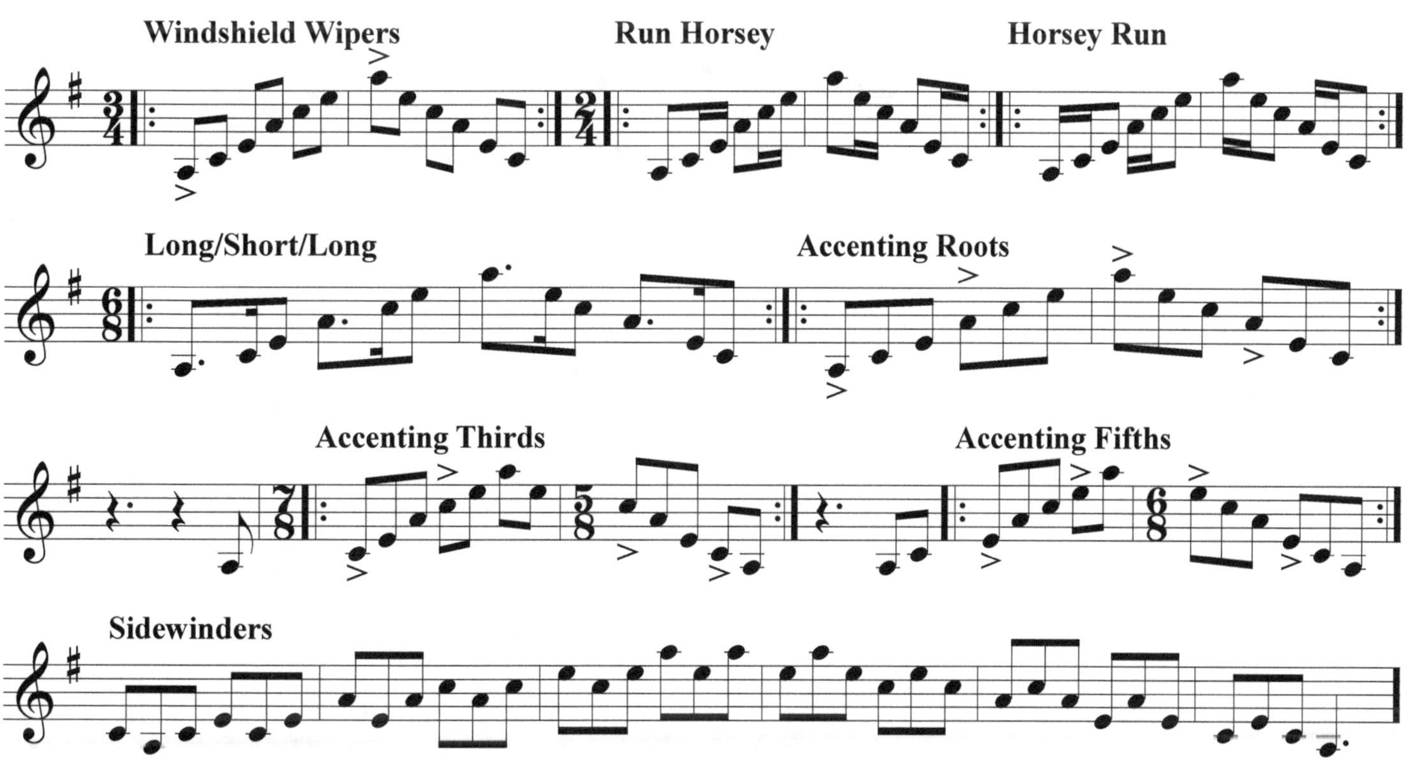

Four by Fours

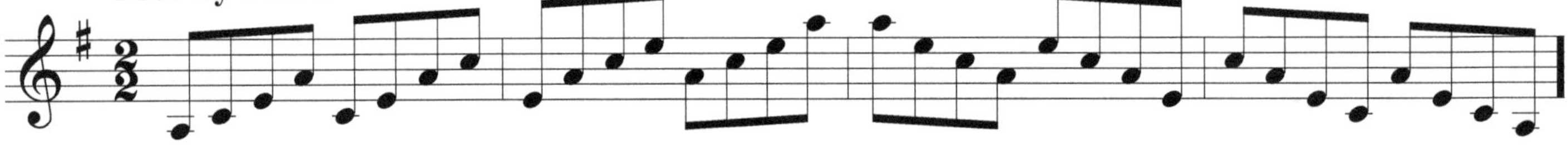

D Minor

Windshield Wipers **Run Horsey** **Horsey Run**

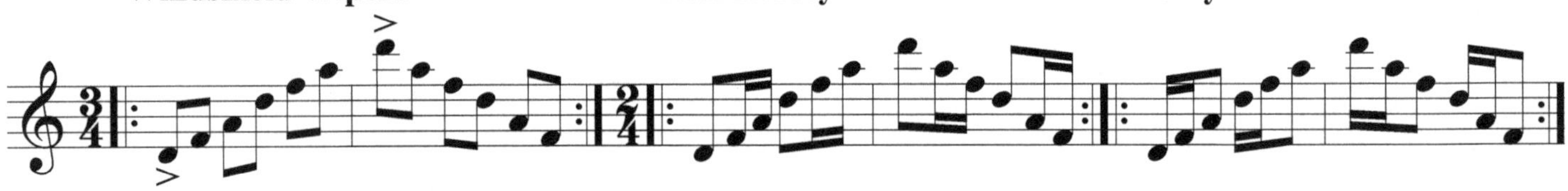

Long/Short/Long **Accenting Roots**

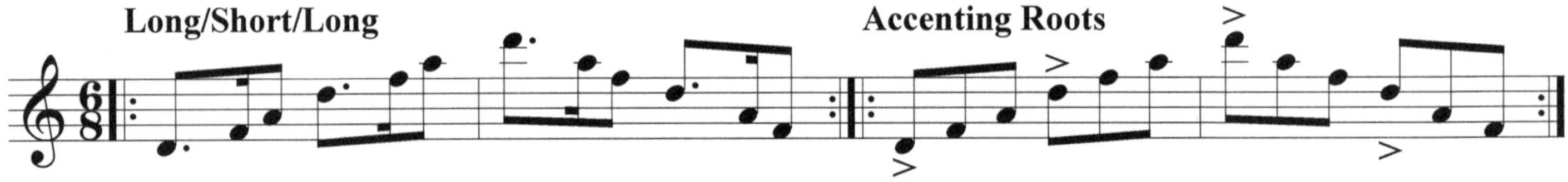

Accenting Thirds **Accenting Fifths**

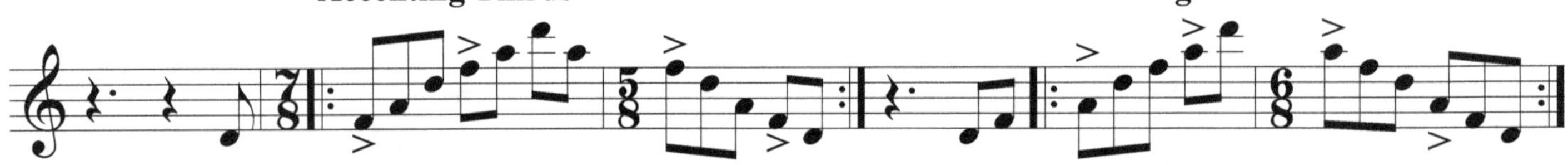

Sidewinders

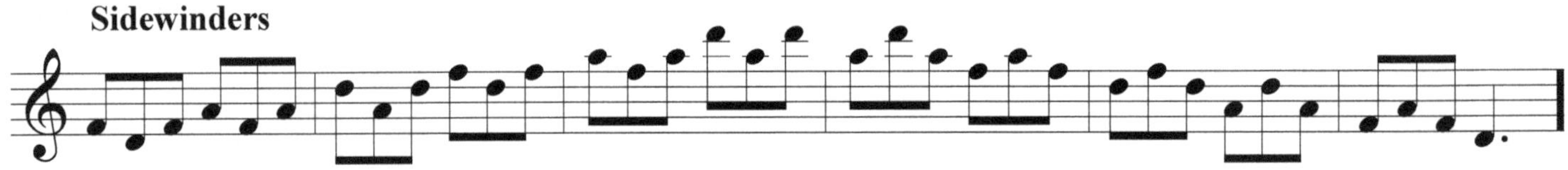

Four by Fours

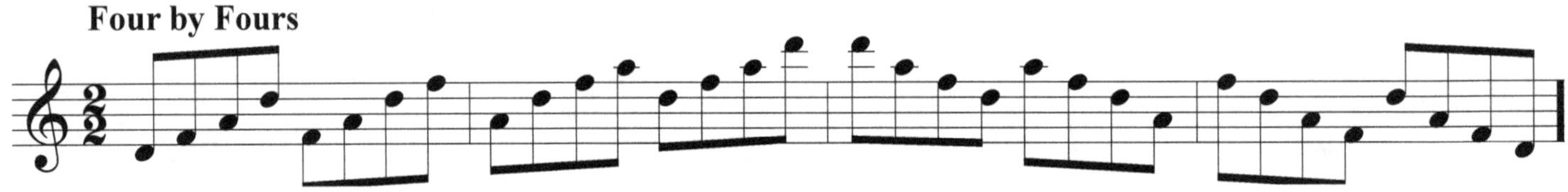

3 Octave Arpeggios: Extended range instruments have even more 3 Octave arpeggios possible and can apply these flowing patterns to them as well.

D Major

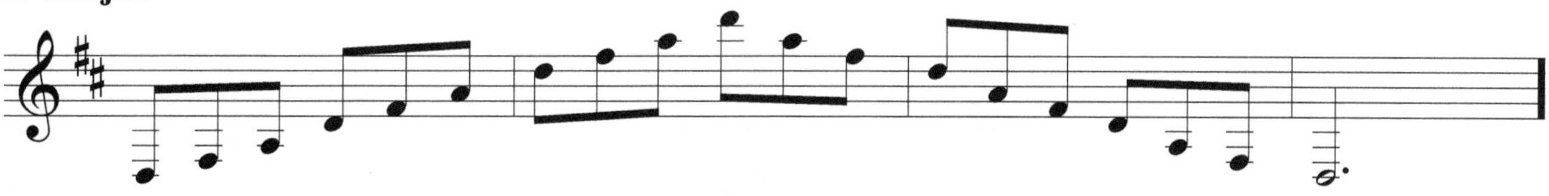

G Major

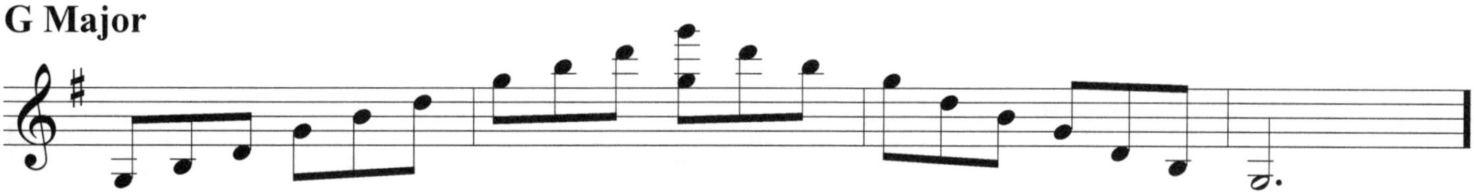

E Minor

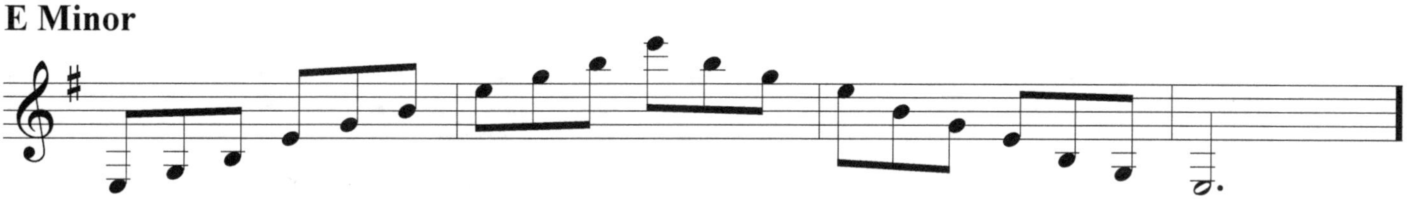

D Maj. 7

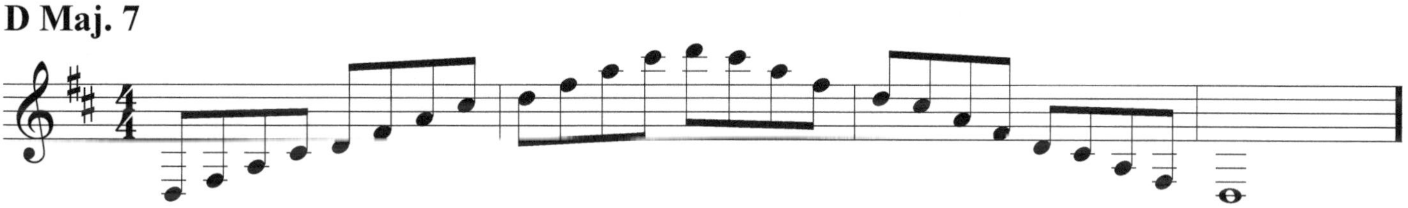

D7

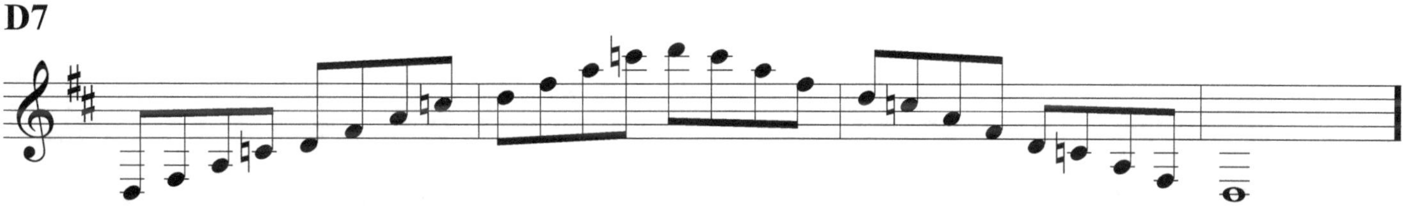

D6

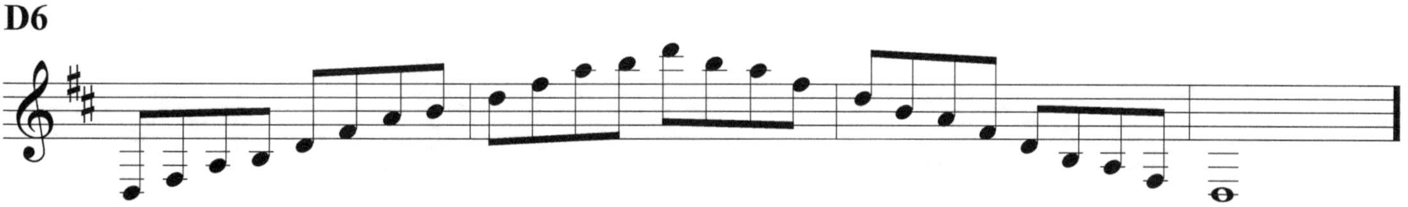

D sus.

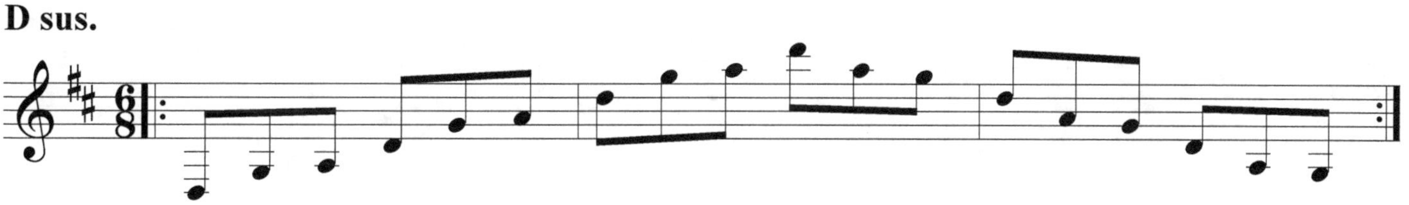

*A sus chord is short for "suspension." These chords consist of a root, fourth and fifth. The term suspension comes from the fourth hanging on and "suspending" over what would normally be the third.

Chord Suffixes These exercises take you through the most common chord extensions (7ths and 6ths). The pattern simply lowers the top note of each arpeggio by half steps to create the new sonorities. You should familiarize yourself with the left- and right-handed patterns for all.

Treble Bridge

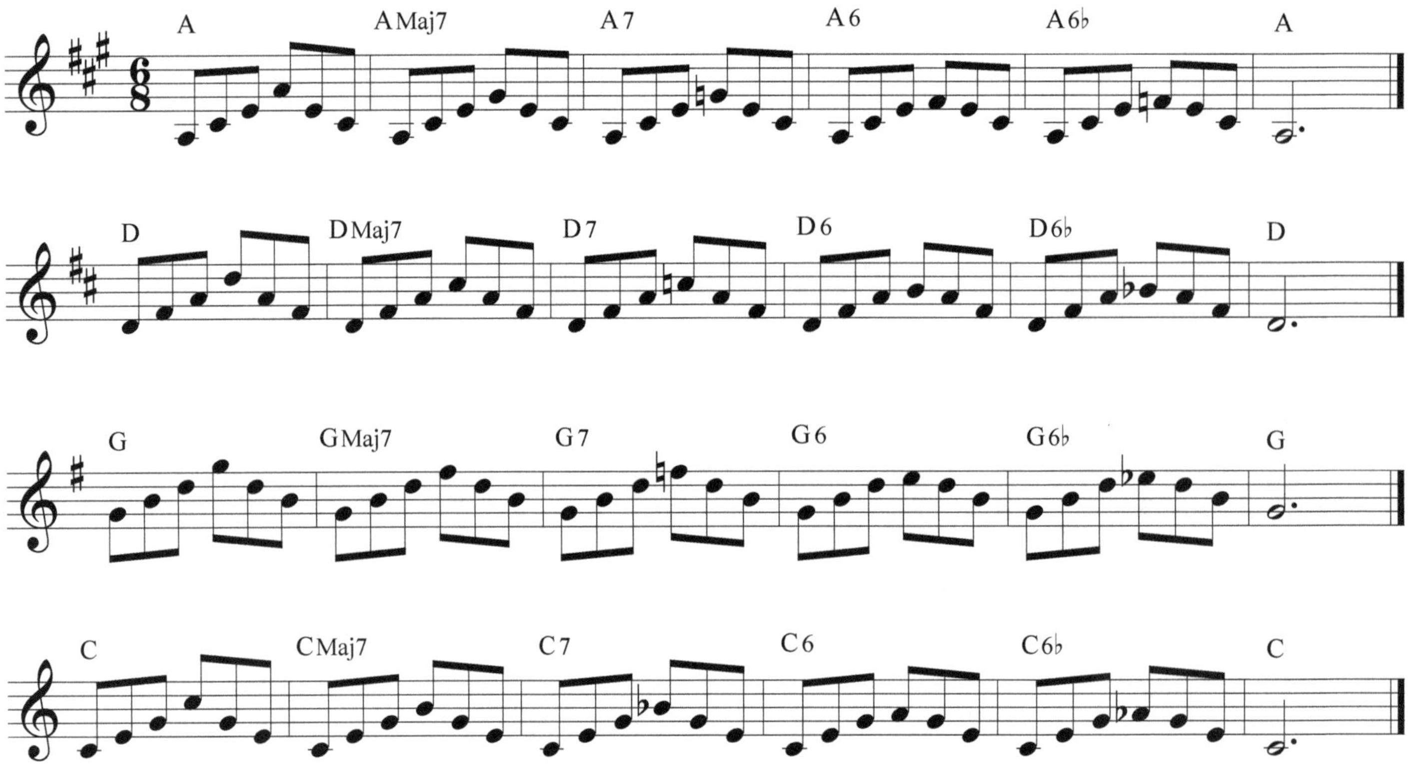

Bass Bridge

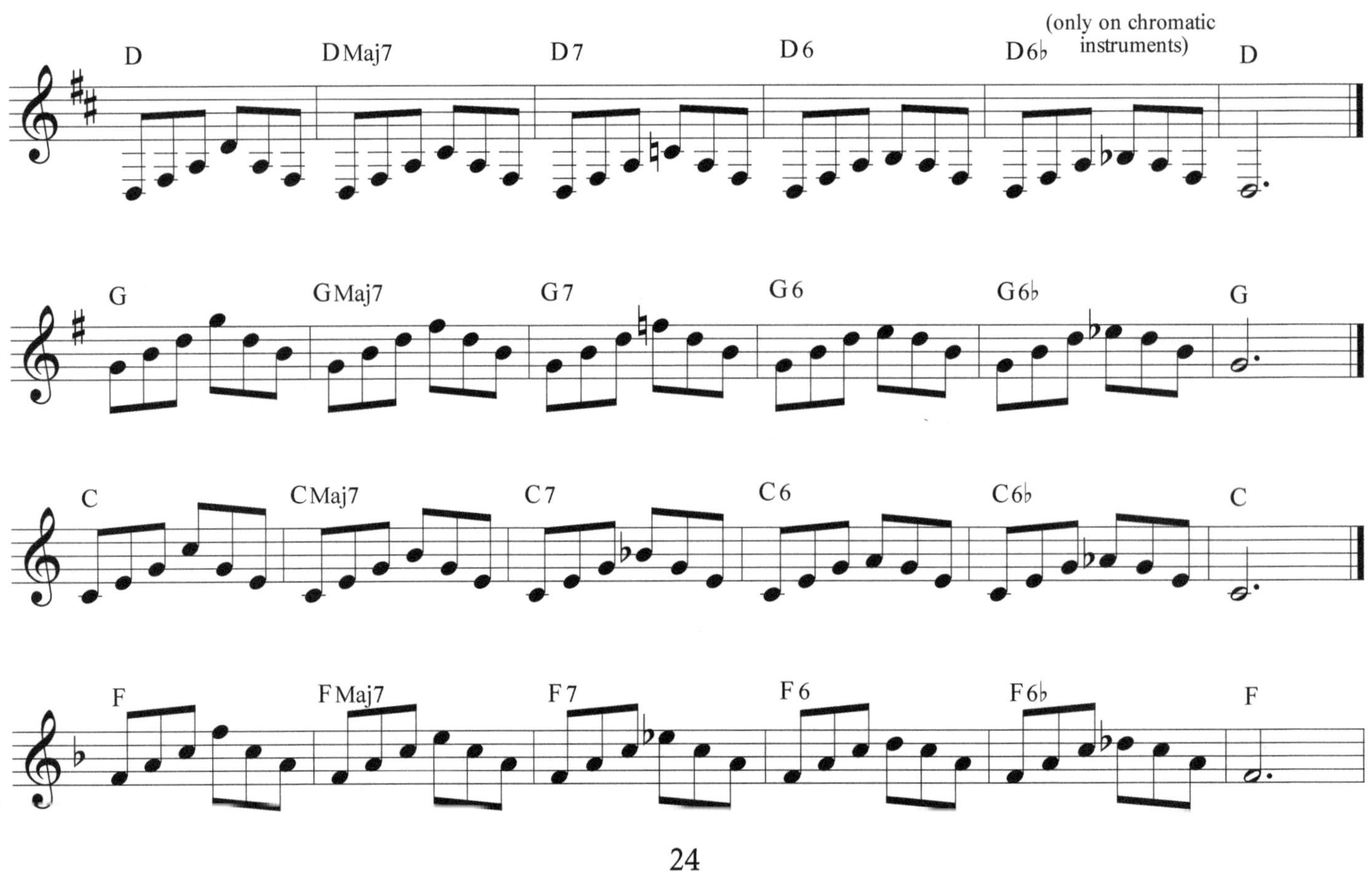

Recordings by Mark Alan Wade

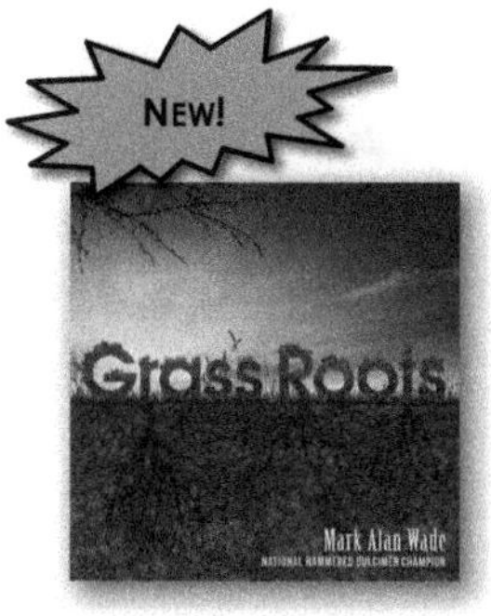

Grass Roots — "I began playing the hammered dulcimer in 1989 and the first songs I learned were traditional fiddle tunes. This is my 7th CD and I am more excited than ever to return to the roots of my dulcimer journey with over twenty years of playing behind me. You will hear influences from the various stops along my dulcimer journey: Classical precision, wild Bluegrass improvisation, progressive New-grass arrangements, and Irish waltzes."
The core of this CD is the *Mark Alan Wade Trio*, comprised of Denison University music faculty members: Andy Carlson (fiddle, mandolin), Casey Cook (guitar) and Mark Wade (hammered dulcimer).

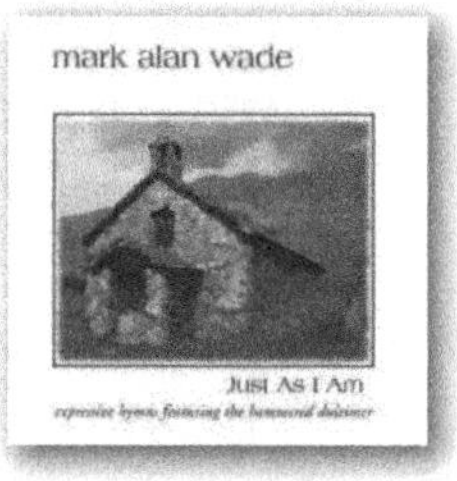

Just As I Am — Mark's second album presents traditional country hymns drawn from diverse musical influences–from blues to classical. This recording features the hammered dulcimer accompanied by varied instruments, including: guitar, bass, mandolin, flute, percussion, fiddle, and vocals on three tracks. Besides *Just As I Am*, the CD includes: *Wayfaring Stranger*, *How Great Thou Art*, *Ave Maria*, *Simple Gifts*, *The Sweetest Gift* and many more.

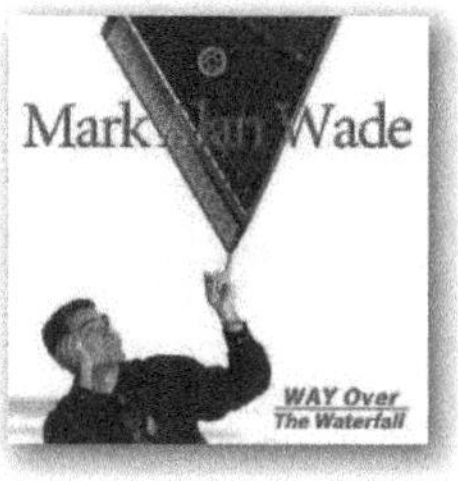

WAY Over the Waterfall — *WAY Over the Waterfall* takes traditional tunes to a new dimension of artistry with jazzy improvisations and tasty embellishments. Featured on this CD is Alex De Pue, 1999 National Fiddle Champion (Winfield, Kansas), Mark Kreis and other great musicians. This CD features great arrangements of: *Billy Bob's Blackberry Blossom Boogie (Blackberry Blossom)*, *Lime Green Sleeves (Greensleeves)*, *Wrongs of Man (Rights of Man)*, *Danny Boyz (Danny Boy)*, *Flight of the Bumble Bee-Bop* and many more.

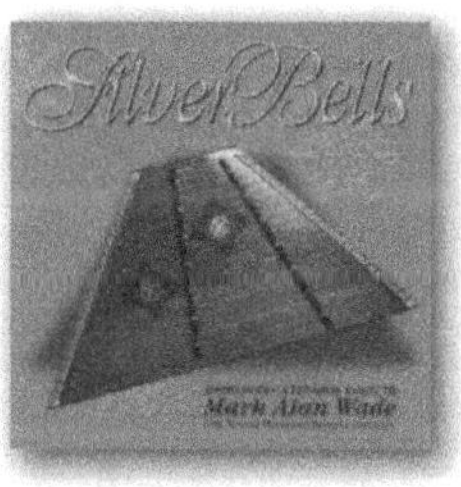

Silver Bells — *Silver Bells*, is a delightful Christmas album filled with instrumental arrangements of holiday favorites. So original! So different! So beautiful! Mark is again accompanied by 1999 Winfield Fiddle Champ, Alex De Pue who frequents the stage of the Grand Old Opry. You will want to play this CD year-round. Includes *Silver Bells*, *Sleigh Ride*, *What Child Is This?*, *Canon in D*, *Joy to the World*, *O Holy Night*, *Winter Wonderland*, *Silent Night* and other Christmas favorites.

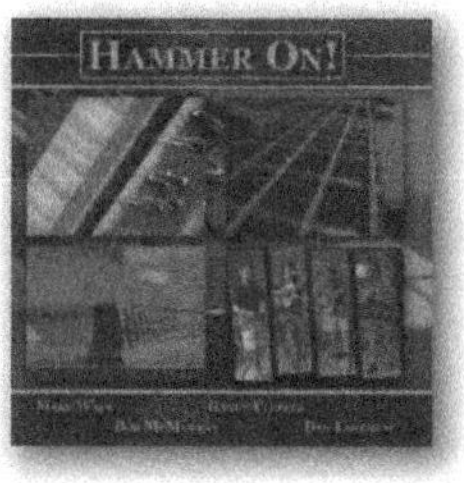

Hammer On! — Mark's ensemble project, *Hammer On!* consists of four multi-instrumentalists – all four play the guitar – all four play the hammered dulcimer – the possibilities are endless! Mark is joined by Dan Landrum, Yanni's renowned hammered dulcimer player, Randy Clepper on cittern, guitar, hammered dulcimer and tenor banjo, and Bob McMurray on guitar and hammered dulcimer. *Hammer On!* music is loaded with an arsenal of driving rhythms and hot licks. Includes: *Rondo in 7/8*, *Enamored*, *Cluck Old Hen*, *Falling Water*, *En Gedi*, *Sweet Georgia Brown* and others.

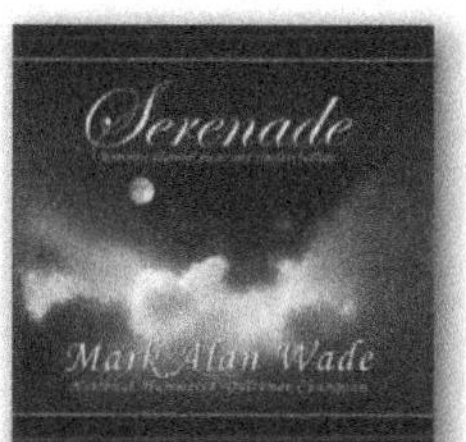

Serenade — Romantic classical pieces and timeless ballads on solo hammered dulcimer. Tracks include: Chopin's *Nocturne, Op.9, no.3*, *Clair de lune* by Debussy, *Prelude from Cello Suite, No.1* by J.S. Bach, *Smoke Gets In Your Eyes*, *The Swan* by St. Saëns, Schubert's *Ave Maria*, *Largo by Rodrigo*, *A Time for Us* (theme from Romeo and Juliet) and many more.

Books

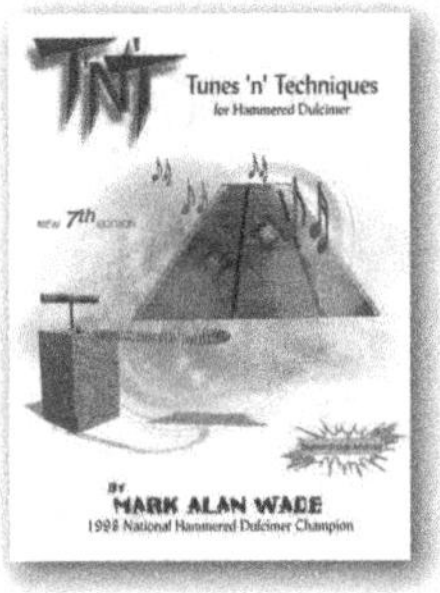

Tunes & Techniques for Hammered Dulcimer — 120 pages. For absolute beginner through Advanced. A Must Have for serious students! There is an optional 80 min. CD.

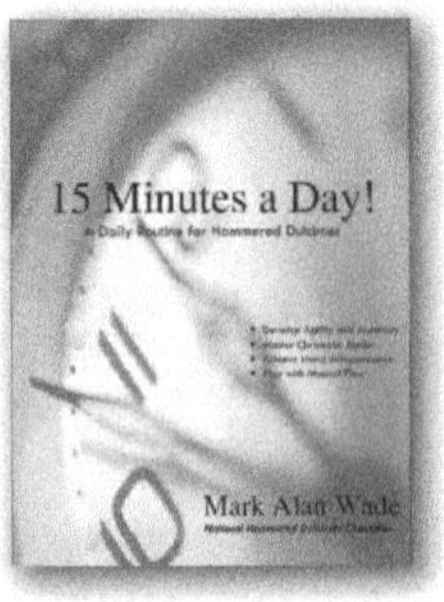

15 Minutes a Day — A daily technique routine book for catapulting your playing to the next level. Assumes you know chords and scales.

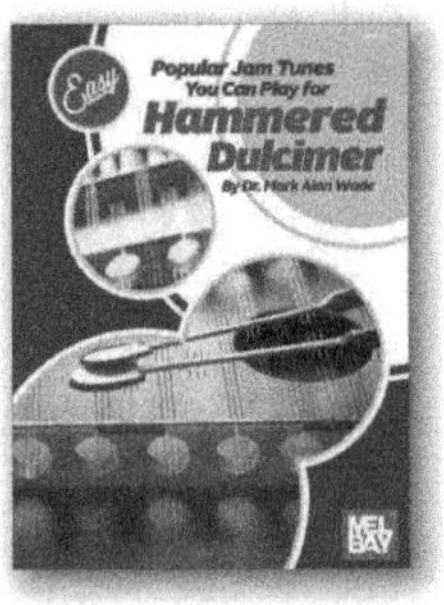

Easy Does It! Popular Jam Tunes — This innovative books presents a treasury of fiddle tunes that you *should* know in two ways—an *easy* version and a *standard* version. This way the book is great for beginners through players who want to grow to be able to play it like I do.

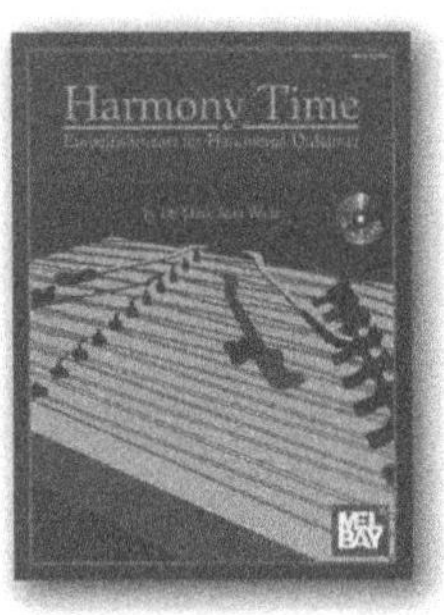

Harmony Time - Embellishments for Hammered Dulcimer — This entire book is dedicated to answering the question: *"How do I add accompaniment and embellishments to melodies on the dulcimer?"* It illustrates how to enhance great tunes to showcase their inherent musicality. Full of illustrations, preparatory exercises and easy-to-play arrangements, *Harmony Time* comes complete with audio CD for aural learners!

WWW.MARKALANWADE.COM

About the Author

National Dulcimer Champion, Mark Alan Wade performs in orchestra halls and music festivals alike with his characteristic mix of classical precision and raw traditional American style. Classically trained as a trumpeter with doctorate and master's degrees in music from The Ohio State University, his unique style emerged as the technique and discipline of his formal training crossed over into his dulcimer playing. He earned his undergraduate degree in music at Ohio Wesleyan University. His performances bring world music to life and revitalize familiar classical pieces on hammered dulcimer.

Mark Alan Wade is based in Northeast Ohio, but his 25+ years performing have taken him all over the U.S., Europe and Asia. In 2013, he was a featured performer and lecturer at the World Cymbalom Congress in Taipei, Taiwan. 2014 found him playing trumpet in an orchestra on the very stages where Beethoven and Haydn performed near Vienna, Austria. Recently he premiered his Irish hymn suite for hammered dulcimer and orchestra, "Streams of Mercy," with the Tuscarawas Philharmonic Orchestra. His upcoming touring schedule includes performances in Los Angeles, Chicago, Orlando, London (U.K.), and Albuquerque. Wade has also performed with the Beach Boys, the Buckinghams, and with numerous orchestras including the Columbus Symphony Orchestra, Mansfield Symphony, Springfield Symphony, Tuscarawas Philharmonic Orchestra, Lima Symphony, Newark-Granville Symphony, and the West Virginia Symphony Orchestra.

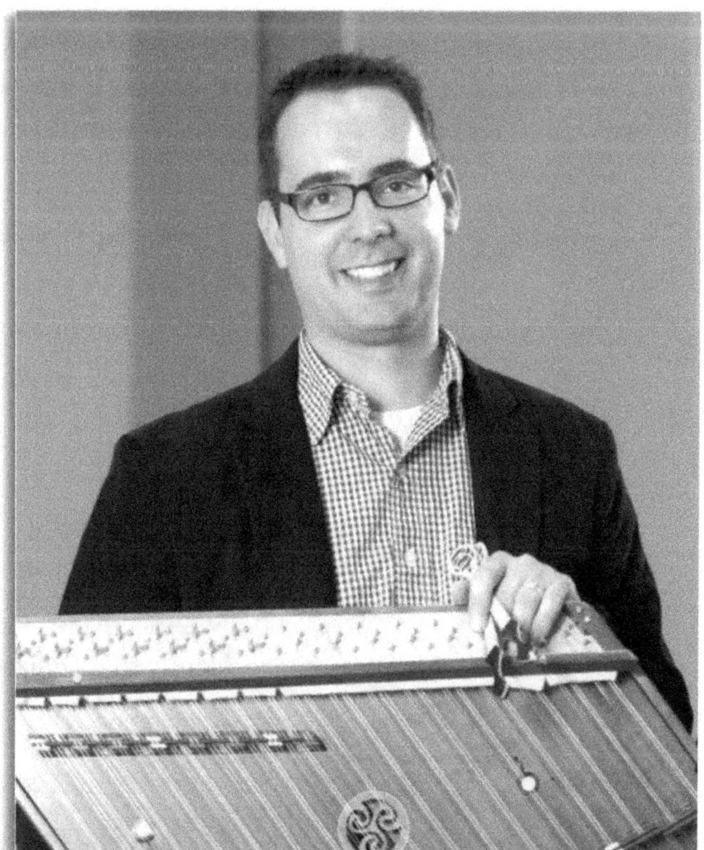

Despite his active performing schedule, he maintains a thriving private studio with six of his students having also won the National Contest for hammered dulcimer. He has held a professorship in trumpet, hammered dulcimer, music theory, and wind ensemble at Denison University.

He has published seven hammered dulcimer CD albums, including *Serenade*, a collection of classical gems for hammered dulcimer. More information can be found at: **MarkAlanWade.com**

Other Mel Bay Hammered Dulcimer Books

Harmony Time: Embellishments for Hammered Dulcimer (Wade)
First Lessons Hammered Dulcimer (Thomas)
Dirt Simple Hammered Dulcimer (Wade)
Hammered Dulcimer for the Young Beginner (MacNeil)
Getting Into Hammered Dulcimer (Thomas)
The Hammered Dulcimer (Hughes)
The Hammered Dulcimer's Companion (Mason)
You Can Teach Yourself Hammered Dulcimer (MacNeil)
A Collection of Original Music for Hammered Dulcimer and Other Instruments (Rizzetta)
A Scottish Christmas for Hammered Dulcimer (Sansone)
An Old English Christmas for Hammered Dulcimer (Thomas)
Ancient Noels (Sansone)
Bluegrass on Hammered Dulcimer (Page)
Celtic Fair (Sansone)
Celtic Meditations (Sansone)
Easy Does It! Popular Jam Tunes You Can Play for Hammered Dulcimer (Wade)
Hammered Dulcimer Arrangements for Special Occasions (Carter)
Hammered Dulcimer Classics (Koenig)
Hammered Fiddle Tunes (Thum)
Maggie's Big Book of Celtic Tunes (Sansone)
Middle Eastern Music for Hammered Dulcimer (Justice)
Scottish Songbook for Hammered Dulcimer (Page)
Shall We Gather: Hymns for Hammered Dulcimer (MacNeil)
Sounds of the Season (Sansone)
The Hammered Dulcimer Treasury of Tunes (Hawley)
The Sandbridge Dance Tune Collection: Arrangements of Reels, Jigs, Hornpipes, Polkas and Rags for the Hammered Dulcimer (Kolodner)
The Sandbridge Waltz and Slow Air Collection: Arranged for the Hammered Dulcimer (Kolodner)
Tis the Season (Page)
With This Ring: A Hammered Dulcimer Collection for Weddings and Special Occasions (Page)
Windrift (Sansone)
Arranging for Hammered Dulcimer (Page)
Hammered Dulcimer Chords (Page)